# THE CONVERSATION OF THE SEXES

# The Conversation of the Sexes,

## Seduction and Equality in Selected Seventeenth- and Eighteenth-Century Texts

ROY ROUSSEL

NEW YORK   OXFORD
Oxford University Press
1986

OXFORD UNIVERSITY PRESS

Oxford   New York   Toronto
Delhi   Bombay   Calcutta   Madras   Karachi
Petaling Jaya   Singapore   Hong Kong   Tokyo
Nairobi   Dar es Salaam   Cape Town
Melbourne   Auckland

and associated companies in
Beirut   Berlin   Ibadan   Nicosia

Oxford is a registered trademark of Oxford University Press.

Published by Oxford University Press, Inc.
200 Madison Avenue, New York, New York 10016

Library of Congress Cataloging-in-Publication Data
Roussel, Roy.
The conversation of the sexes.
Bibliography: p. Includes index. 1. Women in literature.
2. English literature—Early modern, 1500–1700—History and criticism.
3. English literature—18th century—History and criticism.
4. Laclos, Pierre Ambroise François Choderlos de, 1741–1803.
Liaisons dangereuses. 5. Sex role in literature. I. Title.
PR409.W65R68   1986   820′.9′352042   85-15338
ISBN 0-19-503659-X

Printing (last digit): 9 8 7 6 5 4 3 2 1
Printed in the United States of America

TO MAURYA

# Acknowledgments

I would like to acknowledge at least some of the people who have contributed to this project. My greatest thanks go to two friends at SUNY/Buffalo, Bill Warner and Tom Kavanagh. They always seemed to know more about what I was up to at any given time than I did, and I would have been lost without them. Dick Fly, Diane Christian, and Neil Schmitz read various sections of this manuscript and provided valuable suggestions. In this connection I would like to thank particularly Richard Macksey, whose encouragement I appreciated greatly. It is a cliché to say that they are responsible for whatever is valuable in this book. In this case, however, it is the truth.

R.R.

# Contents

# THE CONVERSATION OF THE SEXES

# Introduction

THOSE WHO HAVE WRITTEN for a long time about a single subject know that their perspective changes radically during the process. At first you see your topic the way a mountain climber first views his objective: distant, but a single shape, whole and complete. Then, during the process of writing, you experience it as a succession of immediate situations which require more or less energy and technical expertise. Frequently during this period all you can see of the mountain is the tiny area of the cliff face two inches from your nose. Finally, when you reach the top, the mountain is just a place you happen to be standing while you look at something else.

At this point you realize you have to write an introduction which reproduces your first, all-encompassing vision and at the same time implies all the detailed information you have accumulated in the process of climbing. This seems, really, an invitation to compose a version of those cheap postcards of scenic vistas in which the colors have been enhanced so they are a little too bright and the major features have been penciled in so they are defined with unnatural clarity. In order to avoid as much of this as possible, I would like to forgo any elaborate summary of my argument and limit myself to as concise a statement of my subject as I can, together with a few general comments on the approach I have taken.

To begin, I should explain a choice which is basic to my discussion and which anyone who writes on these works must make. On the one hand, they are all characterized by the centrality of female characters. Although only two—*Fanny Hill* and *Pamela*—bear these characters' names as titles, all are dominated by the figures of women: Mme. de Merteuil and Mme. de Tourvel in *Les Liaisons dangereuses,* and the reluctant heroines of Congreve's comedies. All are, to use Nancy Miller's term, "femocentric" works, and for that reason they have been central to recent feminist discussions of the novel.[1] Though these books are *about* women, however, none of them are *by* women. They do not record women's experience but rather men's conception of this experience.

In *The Heroine's Text* Miller offers one way of approaching this situation. Writing on several of the same novels I have selected, she remarks that they interest her "primarily as the locus of cultural commonplaces about women's identity and women's place, and as an occasion to read the ideological subscript of *literary* femininity in the eighteenth century."[2] She chooses, in other words, to emphasize their status as historical documents which provide insights into the actual conditions of eighteenth-century life and, in this way, most easily finds those places where their representation of women and the real conditions of women's lives coincide.

It is important to understand that I have taken the opposite approach. I have chosen to emphasize that these books are written by men. In this context their "femocentricity" takes on another quality. It appears to be a result of their authors' attempts to question certain areas of their experience which, in terms of conventional oppositions, is feminine. By the conventional opposition between masculine and feminine I do not mean, obviously, the biological difference between male and female. I mean instead those qualities and experiences—masculine control and unity versus feminine submissiveness and fragmentation, for example—which are usually assigned to male and female, respectively, but which in some way can be experienced by both men and women.

One obvious question raised by this issue has to do with the extent to which a man's access to feminine experiences and a woman's to masculine experiences allow each sex to know the other. This is the question posed in various forms by each of the works I have chosen and, consequently, by my own discussion. One apparently reasonable answer would be to say that the qualities considered masculine/feminine define a range of experience which is potentially open to both men and women but that their "natural" access to this range has been blocked by the way society arbitrarily assigns masculine qualities exclusively to males and feminine qualities to females. If this were true, once this fatal confusion between male/female, on the one hand, and masculine/

feminine, on the other, were demystified, then each sex could share the other's experience. Men and women could understand and speak to one another unaffected by their difference.

This is an attractive assumption. It is particularly attractive to several of the authors I discuss, and at some points it might seem that it is mine, too. It is not. Anyone who follows my discussion to its logical end will see that it leads in another direction. Consequently, I want to emphasize that when I use the term "feminine" I am referring to the way in which men experience the difference between masculinity and femininity. I am not pretending to speak for the way women experience this difference. In particular, this is true even when, for example, I discuss the feminine quality of pleasure in Cleland's *Fanny Hill*. The reference here is not by way of the female character, Fanny, to women in general. It is to the man who wrote the book and the men who read it. By the same token, when this experience of femininity is extrapolated to create the perspective of a female character in these works—Pamela, Mme. de Merteuil, or the women in Congreve's plays, for example—I do not assume that this character has any authority to speak for women. They can never be more than men's imagination of women's experience.

I hope that readers will keep this in mind. If not, they will be very confused and, at other times, no doubt, very angry.

My discussion of these works concentrates on two related moments. The opening chapters on Donne and Cleland are about the experience of pleasure as a form of interruption. Here the opposition between masculine and feminine is played out as a conflict between two ways in which the man is given his body and, through it, the world. The masculine is associated with experiences of unity found in an identification with the coherence of a meaning or a visual image. This is the subject who walks through the world with his eyes open and whose speech enacts the power of language to define. The feminine appears at the moment when pleasure fragments this unity and destroys this identification. At this point the man finds himself in the loss of this coherent sense of position and unity. He discovers himself in a feminine experience of disruption, in the multiplicity of particular, heterogenous pleasure which can never be integrated to form a whole.

He becomes, in other words, his own opposite. After this, sexual difference for him is never fixed and external. Whether a man accepts or rejects this experience, inevitably it opens up within him a sense that he contains his own opposite—a sense of self-difference—which qualifies his relationship to a woman. When he looks at her, he no longer sees a simple other across the conventional difference between the sexes. He finds something within himself which *seems* to escape this difference and to correspond to her. In fact, during certain moments of intense emotional pleasure—B's speechlessness before Pamela is a good example—he becomes simply her effect.

Given this awareness, it is only "natural" that a man will talk to a woman in a different manner. No matter what direction his conversation takes—and it can, of course, become an attempt by the man to reestablish his mastery—it will attempt to extend this sense of a relationship outside conventional difference. The last three chapters on Richardson's *Pamela*, Laclos's *Les Liaisons dangereuses*, and the comedies of William Congreve all concentrate on various forms of this conversation. In particular, the chapters on *Pamela* and *Les Liaisons dangereuses* are about exchanges which seem to establish a certain equality between a man and a woman: the exchange of Pamela's journal and B's letter; the correspondence between Valmont and Merteuil. These readings are about the desire for a perfect equality of sympathy or understanding and the inevitable conflict between the private language of these exchanges and the larger circulation of public language, which asserts and enforces conventional differences. The last chapter on Congreve discusses the relation between lovers who find themselves in situations where their opposition has a certain inevitability to it.

In short, from my perspective the subject of these works is that area of ambivalence which is created between a man and a woman when his sense of the fixed opposition of their sexual identities is put into play. This area encompasses the erotic—or one aspect of the latter—a place where pleasure establishes a certain reciprocity between masculine and feminine which seemingly enables them to meet on equal terms. It also includes the romantic, where the intensity of feeling promises to extend this reciprocity to a point where it can be verbalized and acted out. In both cases, what is offered seems to be a relationship which is more equal and more intimate than the opposition of the sexes allows.

In this sense, these works are about the status of personal feeling and expression. The attraction which B feels for Pamela or Valentine for Angelica is not simply the desire of men for women, that is, it is not a reaction to conventional values of beauty, which it is possible to experience several times a day without being disturbed in any real way. Instead, it is a response to signifiers of an individual and idiosyncratic desire which transforms their lives because it will not accept the distances and differences of ordinary existence. By the same token, this is not a desire which will accept the terms of normal conversation. It searches for some ideal exchange which will return the lover to himself complete and whole, an exchange with another who, in the perfect coincidence of question and answer, becomes, in fact, no longer other.

At this point I would like to acknowledge a certain dynamic which affects both the development of these personal exchanges as well as my discussion of them. While this book is, in large part, about conversations, it is not in itself a personal expression in quite the same way. But I obviously do mimic my subject. I accept a certain feminine aspect of experience and develop out of this a relationship with these works which tries to recognize and address the other. The first chapter on Donne's "The Flea" is a good example of this parallelism. In it I interpret a poem in which, traditionally, only the man's voice has been heard and attempt to open up the space where the woman acts. I try to make it a conversation between equals, and it can easily be read as an invitation to engage in the same kind of exchange.

At the same time that my discussion offers "understanding," however, it clearly involves a reappropriation of these novels to men's discourse in a way that is all too traditional. In this, again, I am simply reenacting a common pattern in these works: Valmont abandons himself to his feelings for Mme. de Tourvel only to abandon her, in turn, to his reputation; B surrenders his position as Pamela's master only to reassert himself as her husband. In each case, the expression of feeling which begins in acceptance and surrender and moves to free itself from the conventional relationship of the sexes only succeeds in reestablishing the relationship in another form. So, by the same token, my discussion closes itself only to become a book circulating in a largely male academic world where, from a certain perspective, its sole effect is to make the feminine a moment in the male reader's drama, a phase he is going through, with these novels once more only regarded as stories about women that men tell one another. What is lost in all this, ironically, is the aspect of these works dealing with the real situation of women and, in addition, any sense of the other to whom this understanding is addressed.

Much of the analysis in the last three chapters in particular is devoted to the logic that governs this recuperation. Here it need only be said that it is in no sense a question of a simple misunderstanding but has to do with the way any inequality—particularly one as pronounced as that between men and women—structures the relationship between speaker and listener. For this reason, it is not something that can be explained in a few words. It is, instead, an inevitable consequence of my discussion, a consequence which muddies and corrupts my intention and shows me that my words have said and done things I was not conscious of.

While I cannot avoid this consequence, I would like to say something in the way of a warning concerning one of its possible effects. The awareness that some form of reappropriation limits any personal expression of understanding or sympathy might suggest to readers that these works are about a movement between two opposing positions. On the one hand would be those who surrender to their feelings and speak them naively, without any awareness of the contradictory effects of their words and actions, which lie outside the narrow limits of their conscious intention. On the other would be a group of listeners who know that any attempt to speak across a difference will simply reinforce this difference, and who find in this knowledge the power to put their feelings behind them. The lesson of these works, then, would lie in the progress from the former, mystified, position to the latter, informed, one.

This is a seductive interpretation. But it would be a mistake to accept it. If these works are in some sense written against an innocent belief in the power of feeling and expression, then they are also written against the possibility of any sort of informed transcendence. Their worlds are governed by the twin inevitabilities of distance and desire. The first dictates that the conversation between lovers will never be concluded in a simple understanding, the second that this conversation cannot be refused.

Because these characters will find themselves in a desire for another who is their opposite, their difference, they have no choice but to discover, seduce, or force from the other some response which will allow the part of them which is this desire to live. Consequently, they must enter an exchange in which nothing they say and nothing that is said to them is ever clear, in which they are presented with a bewildering succession of contradictory statements, signals, innuendos, and connotations which can never be concretized to form a coherent meaning. The endless interpretation of this exchange is the labor they perform in the service of their desire. For me the most interesting and valuable aspect of these works is the insight they provide into the necessity and conditions of this labor.

It should be clear by now that this book is not an attempt to develop an all-encompassing theory of desire intended to liberate or resolve. For this reason I have developed the chapters as a series of readings of individual works so that the discussion develops as a response to the imagination of specific situations rather than at a more general level of commentary. A similar consideration has influenced the order of chapters. I did not arrange them chronologically since this would have implied a historical narrative describing the origin of the novel by way of the sonnet sequence and Restoration comedy. Instead, the individual readings follow one another according to the way one possible conversation between a man and a woman might develop. There is an obvious logic to this progression, from the discussion of pleasure in the opening chapter on Donne to the analysis of the witty argument which closes the final chapter on Congreve. But, again, I would not want to favor this order by implying that the moment of this argument in any way represents a conclusion that somehow resolves or escapes the opposition between the two. I do not believe it does. It is possible to arrange these chapters in a number of ways, but any sequence would finally end up telling a story and so would have seemed to privilege one or another moment. With this in mind, I told the story which, at the time I wrote the manuscript, was most important and interesting to me.

# I

## Women and Fleas:

## The Argument of Seduction

### THE FLEA

Mark but this flea, and mark in this,
How little that which thou deny'st me is;
It sucked me first, and now sucks thee,
And in this flea our two bloods mingled be;
Thou know'st that this cannot be said
A sin, nor shame, nor loss of maidenhead;
 Yet this enjoys before it woo,
  And pampered swells with one blood made of two,
  And this, alas, is more than we would do.

Oh stay, three lives in one flea spare,
Where we almost, yea, more than married are.
This flea is you and I, and this
Our marriage bed, and marriage temple is;
Though parents grudge, and you, w'are met,
And cloistered in these living walls of jet.
 Though use make you apt to kill me,
  Let not to that, self-murder added be,
  And sacrilege, three sins in killing three.

Cruel and sudden, hast thou since
Purpled thy nail in blood of innocence?
Wherein could this flea guilty be,
Except in that drop which it sucked from thee?
Yet thou triumph'st and say'st that thou
Find'st not thyself, nor me the weaker now;
 'Tis true, then learn how false fears be:

> Just so much honor, when thou yield'st to me,
> Will waste, as this flea's death took life from thee.

A discussion of Donne's *Songs and Sonnets*,[1] particularly one which is centered on "The Flea," might seem like a strange choice to begin a book which juxtaposes, however loosely, Renaissance love poetry, Restoration comedy, and eighteenth-century novels. The obvious logic of this juxtaposition lies in the way it seems to trace the metamorphosis of the couple from star-crossed lovers to married companions. This arrangement, then, inevitably invokes, to some extent, the whole domestication of romantic love which has recently been documented by Lawrence Stone and Jean Hagstrum, and suggests an approach in which the novel appears to develop from Renaissance love poetry in response to a world in which, increasingly, romantic love had to be incorporated into the demands of everyday life.[2]

It is from just this perspective, however, that the choice of Donne seems a strange one. His *Songs and Sonnets* lacks the emotional consistency—and the continuous narrative quality—of more traditional collections such as Sidney's *Astrophel and Stella* or Spenser's *Amoretti*. In these poems the woman is more or less a fixed mark whose consistency determines the stability of the poet's desire. These collections imply a fairly clear story in which love moves directly toward its given object. This consistency is in sharp contrast to the bewildering succession of attitudes in Donne's poetry.

The issue here has to do with the unifying effect which narrative imposes on diversity by making moments of opposition stages in some logical and dramatic progression toward completion. A certain tradition of Donne criticism does, in fact, impose such a narrative unity on the *Songs and Sonnets* by reading poems such as "The Flea" as the expression of a youthful affectation of cynicism which leads to, and is resolved by, the later, "mature" love poems. Herbert Grierson is the first of a number of critics who locate Donne's achievement in those lyrics—"The Good-morrow," "The Sun Rising," "A Valediction: forbidding mourning"—which celebrate the joys of a contended, mutual love that naturally completes the lover's desire.[3] Although other critics who read the same story in Donne's collection—Helen Gardner, Arnold Stein,

Wilbur Sanders—might disagree with Grierson on specific points, such as his emphasis on married love or the biographical context he imposes on the poems, all would agree that these poems represent the conclusion of Donne's love story.[4]

But in a real sense the *Songs and Sonnets* can be read as criticism of just this kind of narrative. These poems do not come to us numbered and ordered in a fixed sequence which would inevitably privilege these mature poems.[5] The moments of reciprocal love in which the woman and the poet "complete" one another are scattered throughout the collection in a way that puts them in a constant opposition with other experiences which question this vision. In "Farewell to Love" the lover's fascination with the woman is like a child's fascination with a toy. It is a mystification, not a revelation. In this poem her desirability is not intrinsic. It is the desirability of "things . . . coveted by men, / Our desires give them fashion" (ll. 8–9). From this perspective the "all" the lover sees in the woman is like the "all" represented by the globe in "A Valediction: of weeping." Here a workman constructs a figure of the world by taking the "nothing" (l. 13) of a blank sphere and covering it with maps. The lover's image of the woman as his fulfillment, then, is like this globe which images "*All*" (l. 13) the world, only an image which he imposes on her. In reality she is like the blank sphere itself. She is nothing. She is simply natural, in the words of "Love's Alchemy," "Mummy, possess'd" (l. 24).

Another tradition of Donne criticism, in turn, privileges such moments of cynical disillusionment. For C. S. Lewis and J. E. V. Crofts they express Donne's medieval sensibility and his real distaste for women.[6] But to do this is simply to reverse Grierson's story and make cynicism the final, hard-earned wisdom of the experienced lover. And this narrative is open to a similar criticism. There is no reason, in this collection, to value moments of detachment over moments of sincere love. The attempt to trivialize the woman, to make "Changed loves . . . but changed sorts of meat" ("Community," l. 21) never crystallizes into some final vision which allows the men in the *Songs and Sonnets* to master the woman and control their desire for her. As frequently happens in life, statements of detached and ironic wisdom lead "naturally" to moments of the most naive acceptance of desire. "I am two fools, I know / For loving, and for saying so / In whining poetry; / But where's that wiseman, that would not be I, / If she would not deny?" ("The Triple Fool," ll. 1–5).

Rather than attempting to fix this play of attitudes by privileging one moment as its inevitable conclusion, it might be more reasonable to accept the conflict and play between the two. The *Songs and Sonnets* thus becomes the record of an endless argument between the man and the woman. In this argument the man is continually trying to fix her position—to mythologize her as the icon of his own meaning, to dismiss her as the simply fashionable, to trivialize her as the source of a natural but occasional pleasure. But the nervous succession of attitudes in this collection suggests the difficulty of this task. The woman never speaks in these poems. She never answers the poet's language. But she exists as a presence which somehow exceeds and discomposes each formulation, renders the man's language inadequate to fix her as the image of fulfillment, as the conventionally fashionable, as the merely natural.

The following discussion is an attempt to address the terms of this argument. For my purpose "The Flea" is a particularly appropriate poem because for Donne it is precisely this ability to escape the rules of men and to provoke beyond reason that fleas and women have in common.

The Learned are so well acquainted with the Stars, Signs and Planets, that they make them but Characters, to read the meaning of the Heaven in his own forehead. Every simple fellow can bespeak the change of the *Moon* a great while beforehand: but I would fain have the learnedst man so skillful, as to tell when the simplest Woman meaneth to vary. Learning affords no rules to know, much less knowledge to rule the minde of a Woman: for as *Philosophy* teacheth us, that *Light things do always tend upwards,* and *heavy things decline downwards;* Experience teacheth us otherwise, that the disposition of a *Light* Woman, is to fall down, the nature of women being contrary to all Art and Nature. Women are like *Flies* which feed among us at our Table, or *Fleas* sucking our very blood, who leave not the most retired places free from their familiarity, yet for all their fellowship will they never be tamed or commanded by us.[7]—"A Defence of Woman's Inconsistancy"

"THE FLEA" IS A POEM about a man's attempt to convince a woman to sleep with him. Most obviously, then, it is a poem about the language of seduction and, initially, the reader cannot fail to be impressed by the force of this language. The speaker seems absolutely articulate, able to change his tone and the terms of his argument to meet any situation. The man is playing a game of seduction which depends on his agility in maneuvering arguments rather than the truth of any one of them. He proposes a series of meanings for the flea, each of which leads "logically" to the woman's acceptance of his offer, and hopes that she will finally succumb to one of them simply because she will not be able to think of a "logical" reply and will have no choice but to submit. His power is the power of a certain kind of rationality that demands it be answered on its own terms.

The reader who becomes fascinated by the poet's wit will, however, miss much of the poem. The flea becomes, in turn, an image of the mingling of the man and the woman in the sexual act, of their marriage, of the "death" of orgasm; and these abrupt transitions in the poet's argument are not, after all, simply the result of a playful spirit. The man's argument is interrupted or forced to change its terms three times: first by the bite of the flea, which, presumably, interrupts some previous conversation, and then by the action of the woman, whose gesture first threatens and then kills. From this point of view Donne's poem seems to be about the ability of both fleas and woman to somehow stand outside of and oppose the "rules" and "learning" of the speaker's discourse. It would be more accurate to say that this poem is about a conversation in which three elements come into play: the bite of the flea, the discourse of the man, and gesture of the woman. What is the status of each of these?

The existence of the flea itself—which is, after all, the occasion of the poem—reminds us of differences in the conditions of material life in general, and of standards of hygiene in particular, which separate us from the seventeenth century. Donne and his contemporaries were flea-ridden and accepted this as a normal fact of life. Lawrence Stone, in *The Family, Sex and Marriage in England, 1500–1800*, remarks that as late as 1760 Topham Beauclerk, "a man of charm and wit who moved in the highest aristocratic circles," was so filthy that his wife slept in a separate bed.

Yet when ladies at a party complained that he was giving them lice, he replied—totally unashamed—"Are they no nice as that comes to? Why I have enough to stock a parish."[8] We could hardly expect that a hundred years earlier, when standards of hygiene were even more lax, the poet and the woman would be any exception to this condition.

The motif of the flea, of course, has a long history as a rhetorical figure in the sixteenth and seventeenth centuries. Gardner notes, among the many antecedents of this poem, a collection of over fifty verses on fleas in French, Spanish, Italian, Latin, and Greek.[9] But when we read Stone's discussion of the conditions of daily life during this period, we are reminded that fleas were not simply images in a poetic tradition. They were a common and intimate part of existence. From this point of view, Donne's flea is not just a fanciful reworking of a traditional motif. It invokes a certain level of material life, of the facticity of existence. What can we say about it on this level?

First, of course, the flea does not appear. It makes itself felt. The flea's objectivity is marked by the unexpectedness, the aggressive intrusiveness of its bite. This intrusiveness interrupts the poet's thoughts, disturbs the progress of his argument, and focuses his attention on a particular here and now.

In this sense the bite of the flea suggests some original encounter between consciousness and the object. But this encounter is a bite. When the speaker confronts this object, he finds, in its otherness, a part of himself now alienated, foreign. "It sucked me first." The flea's bite, then, is a kind of dismemberment in miniature. It shatters not only the unity of his thoughts but also the wholeness of his body, as this body is the basis for the imagined unity of his self. Here the flea is not simply associated with the material world but, specifically, with a material process involving ingestion, digestion, and expulsion. In this process the unity of the self is always subject to and destroyed by a movement which dissolves it and submits it to differentiation and otherness. The flea evokes a process of orality, but an orality which is clearly different from and opposed to the orality of the poet's language.

The bite of the flea, then, is an encounter with the otherness of the world—not, however, the world of fixed, visible objects, which always reflect us as one of them and assure us of our own unity and visibility. It is, instead, the otherness of a process of assimilation and expulsion in which the "unity" of these objects—and the unity of the poet himself—is continually decomposed and regenerated. This is the way we experience ourselves on particularly hot and humid days, when we drink and perspire so continually and intensely that we become this liquid flow; or when we cut ourselves badly, or vomit, or, of course, lose ourselves in moments of intense sexuality. At these moments we "find" ourselves, paradoxically, in the process of disruption and loss—paradoxically because we discover ourselves fragmented, not in one place. How does the poet react to this intrusion?

The poet marks the flea. His language locates and fixes it, calls attention to its position and visibility. It is no longer something felt but something seen. It becomes an object and, by an extension of this same process, the object is transformed into a metaphor. "Mark but this flea and mark in this, / How little that which thou deny'st me is." This "marking" is strangely contradictory. It seems, on the one hand, to recognize and objectify the otherness and particularity of the flea. But we can see that the poet's language recognizes this particularity only to suppress it. The disruptive otherness of the flea's bite is mastered in the act of naming, defining, transforming, by which it is assimilated into the unbroken continuity of his conversation.

The dynamics of this process—the relationship between the objectification of the flea and its function as a metaphor—are clear in the nature of the poet's images. The outlines of the object define an enclosed space. The flea is self-contained and containing. This enclosure, in turn, becomes the body of the woman, which "swells" with their child, the space of the temple where they are united. The experience of the bite, the physical loss of blood, is recuperated by an act of definition which gives this loss a meaning. When the poet looks at the flea he does not see otherness, his blood transformed and alienated in an insect. He sees himself—his image in the child, his name conferred on the woman. His substance, lost in the bite, is returned to him as meaning.

The association of the body of the flea and the body of the woman in the first stanza points, of course, to the ultimate objectives of the poet's argument. The process by which the poet masters and defines the flea seems only a version—a charming miniature—of the process by which he hopes to master and define the woman. Ostensibly, of course, the poet wants the woman, wants to have her, wants the moment of sexuality she can give. But, curiously, he trivializes the loss of orgasm at the same time he trivializes the flea's bite—"How little that which thou deny'st me is." Instead, his images focus on the recuperation of this loss in images of parenthood and marriage. For him seduction is a process which looks beyond the immediacy of the sexual. It seeks the loss of orgasm only for the time beyond this moment when the woman, too, will be fixed and objectified, when she will bear his image.

When the man compares the flea to a marriage temple and describes the two of them "cloistered in these living walls of jet," he is not, obviously, proposing marriage. He simply wants to present his intentions to the woman in an image which will deflect her negative gesture and make acceptance seem the only reasonable choice. The force of the image does not lie in its explicit reference to marriage but in the way this reference sanctifies the poet's attempt at mastery. It is an expression, really, of what Donne in his sixteenth elegy calls "my words masculine persuasive force."[10] The vision of the poet and the woman enclosed in the flea defines the experience of mastery which comes with the successful exercise of this power. In his moment of triumph both the woman and the flea reflect the man, mirror his meaning. He lives in a world he has composed.

As in all of the *Songs and Sonnets,* the women in these poems meet the man's argument with silence. At first glance it would seem that they accept their subjection to his language and pass silently from the name of their father to the language of their seducer. But it would be a mistake always to equate this silence with a simple passivity or acquiescence. Often, in these poems, it masks some powerful effect on the poet, some action or influence, which the poem is written to suppress or deflect. Think, for example, of "A Valediction: of weeping." Here the woman's tears are silent, but they threaten to provoke the poet's own, to destroy his composure, to "draw . . . up seas to drown me" (l. 20). The poem is not imposed on a passive silence but is written in response to this provocation. In a similar way, the woman in "The Flea" is silent but not passive. Her gesture is her response, her answer. It does not have the status of the poet's argument. It does not embody an abstract, conceptual message. It is not seen or described directly. It comes from the margin and takes place in the space between verses.

It does, however, have meaning. Like the poet's metaphors, the woman's gesture is a way of marking the flea, of staging it and giving it—in the widest sense of the word—a significance. The gesture is, finally, not directed against the flea itself—the reality of its bite—but against the power of the poet's language to define. Her gesture answers his argument not by naming but by pointing, and in pointing it kills. The woman destroys the (apparent) objective unity of the flea which grounds the poet's images. She does not answer his argument but acts in a way that reverses the process of his definition and reveals the truth his meaning suppresses—the truth of the body as process, the level on which we experience ourselves in the loss and dispersal of our sense of coherence.

The woman, like the flea, draws blood. By this act she rejects his meaning and chooses her own, defining herself in relation to an aspect of experience which is opposed to the poet's language. But this is not a simple refusal. The poem describes a scene of seduction and, like most seductions, this one is mutual. The woman's gesture is itself a counteroffer, a counter-seduction. The obvious association of the bite of the flea and the woman's gesture—they both draw blood—reminds us of the equally obvious association of the dissolution and loss of the bite and the dissolution and loss of orgasm, the pain of the bite and the momentary death of sexuality. The man had offered this moment, but he had offered it in terms of images which transcend it—the stability of meaning and marriage. The woman's gesture, it seems, offers this moment for itself, for the mingling of their "bloods" in an experience of loss which has no necessary reference to any other moment, later, when it will be discussed, given meaning, recuperated.

Implicitly the woman's gesture asks the man to stop talking, to act, to respond to her gesture in kind. But, obviously, if the man accepts this, he accepts the dissolution of the unity of the masculine. In the mingling of the two he will come to reflect the fragmented quality of her experience. In a number of these early poems Donne, in fact, shows a certain fascination with this assimi-

lation of the masculine by the feminine. In "The Indifferent" it is
the woman who demands consistency. But the man, who has
learned the joys of inconstancy from women, refuses and assumes the feminine right to change without reason. "Must I, who
came to travail through you," he asks, "grow your fix'd subject,
because you are true?" (ll. 17–18). Again, in his third elegy
Donne speculates that because "likenesse glues love," his love for
woman will form him in the image of her mutability. "Likenesse
glues love: and if that [change] thou so doe, / To make us like
and love, must I change too?" (ll. 23–24).[11]

At these moments it is the man who abandons the position of
the "fixed subject" and comes to reflect the woman. In one of his
heroical epistles Donne describes a certain kind of sexual experience which corresponds to this assimilation. This poem is supposedly written by Sappho to her lover and for this reason involves an imaginative identification with the feminine. Here the
two lovers image one another. "Likenesse begets such strange
selfe flatterie / That touching my selfe, all seems done to thee"
(ll. 51–52).[12] But in the absence of that object which signs the
unity and significance of one body and its difference from the
other, it is a likeness made of particular differences. "My two lips,
eyes, thighs, differ from thy two, / But so, as thine from one another doe" (ll. 45–46).[13] Here the unity of the body, and of the
subject, is lost in particularity, each part equally singular, equally
different one from another. In the confusion of their mingling,
each part escapes from and becomes greater than the whole. The
joy of their union is the pleasure of this escape, this loss.

The woman's gesture, then, is an offer of herself not as an
image of beauty or meaning but as that which discomposes these
images. It is, of course, silent. It cannot explain itself, and my
exposition of its "meaning," an exposition which obviously suggests certain contemporary definitions of the feminine, could
easily seem as bizarre a conceit as the poet's exposition of the
flea.[14] But it would be a mistake to think that the seventeenth
century was ignorant of these issues. They simply addressed them
in a different language. Reread the passage from Donne's *Paradoxes and Problems* cited in the opening pages of this essay. It is
clear that for Donne the problem posed by the feminine has to do
with the fact that it cannot be fixed or known by the symbolic.

"The Learned are so well acquainted with the Stars, Signs and Planets, that they make them but Characters, to read the meaning of the Heaven in his own forehead . . . [but] Learning affords no rules to know, much less knowledge to rule the minde of a Woman." There is something in the nature—the sexual nature—of women that resists this translation into "Characters" which would allow them to be defined or "ruled" by men. "Philosophy teacheth us, that *Light things do always tend upwards,* and *heavy things decline downwards;* Experience teacheth us otherwise, that the disposition of a *Light Woman,* is to fall down . . . woman being contrary to all Art and Nature."

Yet for Donne it is not the fact that woman is, in contemporary terms, outside the symbolic that is her most disturbing characteristic. It is the fact that in spite of her apparent distance and difference from man, he is, strangely, like her. It is the resemblance which exists, in some way, beneath or alongside their difference which is most troubling. "Women," he continues, "are like *Flies,* which feed among us at our Table, or *Fleas* sucking our very blood, who leave not the most retired places free from their familiarity, yet for all their fellowship will they never be tamed or commanded by us." The man does not find the feminine arrayed against him at a distance, where it can be confronted in a comfortable way. Man finds femininity in the folds and recesses of his own body, in the places where fleas bite.

THE PASSIVITY OF THE WOMAN in "The Flea" is an illusion. She is not simply a silent other waiting obediently to mold herself in the image of the man's language. For Donne she is the location of an active pleasure which is fluid and disturbing, and which argues against his language. Nor is it a pleasure easy for the man to trivialize and dismiss. If he is honest, he must acknowledge the "familiarity" between himself and the woman which is revealed by her gesture. It seems to awaken some identity within him. He feels it intimately. At this moment he seems to join her in an instant of feminine pleasure which is the denial of his masculine voice. The effect of this gesture, then, is to set up an ambivalence in the man's experience of his own masculine nature, to create in him a certain sense of self-difference. And this sense, in turn, demystifies the conventional association of masculine and feminine qualities with male and female gender. This association no longer seems the "natural" and inevitable result of intrinsic anatomical structures but rather simply conventional and arbitrary. It imposes a difference where, in fact, there is none.

From this point of view there are two kinds of seductions. In one the man pretends to love the woman, to be taken by her. He mimics a feminine susceptibility to feeling, emotion, and surrender to pleasure, only to lure her to do the same. Then he tells his friends. He recuperates his surrender as triumph. He has conquered her and added to his reputation, while for her surrender marks inescapable ruin. This is the "work" of seducing and ruining woman which has grown so tedious to Valmont in *Les Liaisons dangereuses*. It is understandable why he feels this way because it is work done in the name of convention. Its effect, finally, is to assert the "inevitable" inferiority of women, their "natural" susceptibility to feeling and emotion, while asserting the independence and superiority of men to women and to the feminine. No matter how much it seems to add to the personal reputation of the seducer, its final effect is not to assert his power but only the traditional power of the masculine. For this reason his triumph will always be impersonal, since it will alienate him from the object of his personal desire: It will establish a difference between himself and that woman in particular who has awakened his interest.

There is, however, another form of seduction which is initially the opposite of this kind of alienating work. It begins the moment the man is touched by a specific woman, when she awakens in him an interest which is undeniably personal—and, therefore, undeniable—but which assumes an intimacy and identity between the two which violates and calls into question their conventional difference. This second form of seduction is generated by the twin possibilities which emerge from the man's realization that the differences which separate him from the object of his desire are merely traditional. The first is the possibility of a truly personal desire, one which can free itself from the conventional relationship of men to women. This is the possibility that he can speak for himself, express not the power of the male/masculine over the female/feminine but voice his intimate feelings for this woman, for those qualities which mark her as the location of his desire and, in doing so, differentiate her from other women. The attraction of this possibility is reinforced by the sense that the man and the woman are not inevitably opposed to one another. Consequently, the man can hope for a union between the two on some terms. He can dream of a satisfaction as intimate and personal as his desire.

In the first kind of seduction, no matter how intensely the man seems to feel and no matter how powerful the woman seems in her ability to inspire such feelings in him, the two merely enact a ritual which will always end by reaffirming their difference. In the second form of seduction, however, it is this conventional difference which is questioned. From the moment the man becomes personally interested, he and the woman *seem* to enter an area "outside" or "beyond" their stereotyped opposition, where the inevitability of this opposition is put into play in the name of a possible identity. Donne's poem dramatizes a situation in which the man and the woman have, presumably, conspired to hide themselves in some secluded corner, away from grudging parents and other guardians of public order. Here they speak or act their feelings directly. Each, of course, tries to seduce the other. They argue. But their argument is a personal one which they will settle between themselves.

In the novels I have chosen, all of the central relationships— Charles and Fanny, B and Pamela, Valmont and Mme. de Tourvel, Mme. de Merteuil and Valmont, Congreve's lovers and his heroines—involve seduction in this second sense. All of these novels, then, are in some sense concerned with the possibility of this kind of private conversation, about our ability to feel personally, to express these feelings and receive a response which escapes the conventional terms of our world. With this in mind, we might speculate on some of the directions this exchange might take; think, in particular, of the various forms of address that are open to the man who wants to give voice to his desire for the woman.

On a first reading, of course, this seems a simple issue. The man voices his desire directly. He demands that she say yes, that she accept his desire as her meaning and respond in an unambiguous manner. In his efforts to speak directly and forcefully, he is again only exercising the masculine prerogative to master the feminine which society grants to men. But he is appropriating this power to himself, exercising it in his own name. Normally, his right to exercise this prerogative is limited, and the distance between himself and the woman maintained, by the codes which tie her to her father. But for the speaker the fact that the woman bears the father's name does not mark some immutable essence. It is a purely accidental designation which can be toyed with and changed. So he can assume this power himself, redefine her, as he redefined the flea, according to his mood and the needs of his argument. He can impose his name. The poem, really, is an exercise in the personal appropriation of this power of definition.

On its most basic level, then, "The Flea" dramatizes the man's attempt to voice his desire forcefully and demand a complementary response from the woman. Here he adopts the role of the undeniably masculine but unconventional outlaw and lover. His desire appears in the strength of his personal will, which carries the woman's resistance before it. At this moment she gives herself to him and answers the question of his desire completely. She becomes his image and joins with him in an equality which will admit no difference.

But on this level the poem also suggests another equally unambiguous approach. Instead of demanding, the man could surrender to her seduction. He could give himself to the effect of her gesture and to the feminine side which it awakens. In this way he would correspond to her, join her in the experience of some force or rhythm which exists "behind" language. Their difference, again, will yield to an identity which is realized when the femininity of the male and that of the female coincide in this moment.

However more or less successful either of these approaches might be in individual cases, they both seem, in principle, clear and uncomplicated. In this they have the apparent simplicity of all strong expressions. But the proof of any form of address is never in the speaker's own sense of certainty and simplicity but in the response it elicits. The efficacy of the man's language or surrender, then, will not lie in the feeling of expressiveness which either may give him, but in the nature of the woman's response, which is, finally, where his message will be defined. The man obviously enjoys his own facility. He likes to hear himself talk. But this enjoyment of his own argument will mean nothing if it does not have the effect he intends on the woman in question. Her response must be a response to him. It must recognize the specificity of his feelings and his expression. And the same will be true, of course, if he abandons himself to her gesture. He wants to surrender to and join her.

If we read the poem with this in mind, we can see how difficult it will be for either a direct statement or enactment of desire to ever receive such an explicit response. Embodying the power to interrupt, the woman's gesture underscores the truth of the marginal, of all that is excluded from the symbolic and not allowed to express itself there. This power is real; it has significance. But this significance is defined by its effects on the symbolic just as the gesture is apparent only in its destruction of the flea and its disruption of the man's argument. The man wants the woman's gesture to be *her* gesture, to express *her* desire for him in a way that will master him and make him over in her own image. Yet her gesture can never be more than its effect. It can never be more than interruption, and the unbound sexuality with which it is associated here can never establish itself as a truth that can be articulated independently of the man's language. So the man will experience it only as another manifestation of the feminine's ability to contradict the masculine. And the more directly the woman acts, the more emphatically she gestures in an attempt to insist that this is *her* desire, the more impersonal it will seem to the man, the more it will appear simply as an expression of the feminine.

But if he speaks, the situation will be essentially the same. The man's position will not be markedly different. Again, he wants the woman's response to be a response to *his* language, not to the conventional power to master and define. And the more loudly or forcefully he argues, in an effort to convince her that it is his desire he expresses, the more the woman will hear in his voice the arrogance of men toward women. She will react to the force of argument itself rather than to the specificity of his argument.

However paradoxical this may seem, it will not be unfamiliar to anyone who has been in a situation which itself signifies desire. This would be true, for example, of any singles bar. To be there means, if you are a man, that you desire a woman, or, if you are a woman, that you desire a man. But this is exactly what makes these locations so problematic and the people in them, for the most part, so uncooperative. The situation bespeaks the general desire of men for women and vice versa. Each man and woman, however, searches for a desire which is for them alone. And it is just this specificity of one person's response to another which is so difficult to establish against the frenzied activity of the seduction of woman by man. Here the least effective approach is usually the most explicit because, however heartfelt it might be, it is usually heard as impersonal and mechanical.

One could say the same thing about a moment in which a woman first finds herself alone with a man. Their privacy evokes desire independently of their intention. It places them in a seductive relation to one another. And it is likely that the more explicit each is with the other, the more each will see in the other's response not himself or herself but a response to the situation and the generalized desire it elicits.

Despite the fact that the man has succeeded in finding a private place to meet the woman, his attempt to speak to her in a direct and forceful way will inevitably be compromised by the ordinary relationship of men to women. This conventional relationship will determine not his intention but rather each individual's understanding of the other's response in such a way that their exchange will lose its personal quality. They will become symmetrically anonymous figures for one another and their conversation will be just another example of the way men talk to women and vice versa.

This initial argument, in which the man hopes to move the woman outside her conventional setting and deal privately with her, only ends with a reenactment of the most stereotyped opposition between the sexes. Yet, however frustrating this encounter is for the man, it could, if he is sensitive and thoughtful, suggest another alternative. This alternative replaces the vision of an immediate identity with the woman with a more abstract idea of mutual understanding. As we have seen, the woman's gesture has revealed the feminine aspect of his experience, and he might reasonably assume that their argument would have had an equivalent effect on the woman by awakening her masculine nature. In this way the apparent failure of their first exchange is recuperated by this experience, which provides a basis for their mutual understanding. The emphasis here falls on how conventions of sexual difference have been internalized by the man and the woman in a way that has led them to repress the other within themselves.

The ideal of understanding which emerges from the man's initial frustration assumes that the conventional restriction of masculine qualities exclusively to the male and feminine qualities to the female is an artificial division imposed on a continuous range of experience which they both—potentially—share. In other words, it assumes that a man's experience of "his" femininity corresponds in some way to a woman's experience of "her" femininity, and vice versa; once both understand the arbitrariness of restricting experience according to the subject's gender and accept the other within themselves, they will "naturally" come to understand one another because their experiences of the world will coincide. They will still live with the difference between masculine and feminine, of course. They will not escape it the way they would have if the man had received a personal response to his initial demand or consummated his relationship with the woman in a surrender which joined the two. But this difference will no longer separate them because each will have access to the other's experience. Their relationship will be characterized by a reciprocity between masculine and feminine which will assure their mutual understanding of one another. From this point of view the man's initial attempts to seduce the woman by choosing either a masculine demand or a feminine surrender seem childlike and naive.

The aggressive argument in "The Flea" seems to lead to such "mature" love poems as "The Sun Rising" and "The Goodmorrow." In these poems the man and the woman's arguments give way to this reciprocity of mutual understanding. The equality they celebrate is not the equality of absolute identity but the more subtle equality which exists between two people who understand one another despite their differences and reflect this understanding in their conversation with one another. In "The Good-morrow," for example, the man offers the woman a vision of the circumscribed world of their love. But it is a circumscription which results from a mutual agreement. In the last stanza of this poem, the lovers are described as equal hemispheres which join to form a closed universe independent of the world around them.

> My face in thine eye, thine in mine appears,
> And true plain hearts do in the faces rest;
> Where can we find two better hemispheres,
> Without sharp North, without declining West?
> Whatever dies, was not mix'd equally;
> If our two loves be one, or, thou and I
> Love just alike in all, none of these loves can die.
>
> (ll. 15–21)

"The Good-morrow" turns on the obvious analogy between the lovers' physical awakening and their discovery of the true nature of their love for one another. The image of the two lovers as opposed mirrors reinforces the essentially visual nature of this experience. The lovers face one another, with the man contemplating his own image in the eyes of the woman. This reflection, in turn, is itself only the image of the sincerity of his feeling, of the "true plain" heart which shows, undisguised, in his face. The abstract and static nature of their arrangement contrasts sharply with the description, in the first stanza, of the world both have left behind. Then, before he was "wean'd" (l. 2) the poet's experience was tactile, immediate, multiple. He "suck'd" (l. 3) on "country pleasures" (l. 3). Then his desire was dispersed in a way that fragmented him, bound him in a relationship to objects which was momentary, immediate, and blind.

Now, however, the infinity of these particular desires is concentrated, raised to the level of the visual. The relation of the lovers to one another is like the relation of facing mirrors or the two halves of a sphere. They find themselves in the unity of their image as reflected in the other. In their union each coincides with this image; together they form a self-contained world where all desire is stilled.

Here the tonality of the man's language is completely different from the overt aggressiveness and argumentativeness of the poet in "The Flea." This man is the sincere, not the masterful, lover. He seems, in some way, to have accepted the terms of her experience. It is the morning after; his language is permeated by the intensity of the feelings they have both shared. It bespeaks these feelings and his acceptance of them. By the same token, the woman apparently accepts his language. She does not react to it as something foreign to her own nature, and her silence does not seem to be the uncooperative silence of the woman in "The Flea." It is simply a voiceless affirmation which answers him, returns his gaze, closes and completes the sphere which contains them.

"The Good-morrow," apparently, is about the ability of sincerity and openness to transcend the differences which separate us, and the most sensitive of Donne's readers have acknowledged this obvious intention in the poem. In the introduction to her edition of Donne's poetry, Helen Gardner finds his greatest achievement in such mature lyrics as "The Good-morrow." In these pieces, she comments, "the 'He and She,' the 'I and Thou' of Donne's earlier poetry are transformed into 'We' and 'Us.' "[15] In this way "The Good-morrow" would define the end toward which love should develop, an understanding which finally resolves the argument of lovers.

Yet these readings, which privilege poems such as "The Good-morrow" and see in them the conclusion of the lover's narrative, have a paradoxical effect. They make it clear how hard it is for even the most sincere statement of openness and understanding to suppress echoes of difference and conflict. These critics emphasize not only the unity of the lovers but the fact that their situation is completely human. Despite its platonic overtones, for Arnold Stein "The Good-morrow" is not a religious vision of the actual transcendence of this world of multiplicity and difference. "What we have," he writes, "is a metaphor, in which the act and the process of imagining are not completely assimilated into the singleness of identification. It is an imaginative translation that knows it is imaginary."[16] The unity it achieves, then, is "a lyric moment in a world of fact."[17] It has the status of a meaning—the expression of an intention which becomes real because the lovers, and the poem's readers, understand and accept it in the same way.

But if the visions of reciprocity and unity produced by the most intense expressions of human love, the passion of romance, and the understanding of marriage are, in fact, only human, then they must exist in a constant conflict with the differences of this world. From this point of view it is easy to see how the second could corrupt the first, how our most private understandings could become reappropriated by conflict, how close the tone of sincerity is to that of a repressive tolerance which intends mastery. This possibility is made most obvious by feminist critics, who have attacked the apparent simplicity of such images as the spheric world of lovers in "The Good-morrow." The union of the man and the woman to form a sphere is a reference to Aristophanes' myth in Plato's *Symposium*, in which love is the result of the splitting of spheric androgynes into two halves that search continually for one another in order to reassume their original shape. The conclusion of the poem seems to describe a unity between the sexes, an equality which is more powerful and fundamental than any difference between them.

But to many of the women who encounter such images the issue does not seem so clear. Marlyn Farwell, for instance, finds an ambiguity in these images between the idea of the fusion of the two and that of their balance. Most critics equivocate, she continues, but "the distinction is crucial."[18] Balance implies the coexistence and reciprocity of two independent principles. Fusion, on the other hand, implies that one principle has subsumed and defined its opposite, creating "one supposedly asexual evaluative quality."[19] Since "the dominant Western concept is fusion" and "the universal is most often identified with whatever is male," this reading of androgyny simply "privileges the masculine."[20]

For Farwell there is something dangerous in the ambivalence of these images, which, on the one hand, attract all our longings for some ideal, paradisiacal state of harmony and, on the other, somehow place them in the service of the traditional domination of women by men. If we read the poem from this point of view, we are less likely to take the sincerity of the lover at face value; we will hear in it the desire of Western society to privilege the masculine. For the moment, Stein says, the two become "one in the image."[21] Yet this is just the point. The unity of the lovers in this poem is the unity of an image imposed on the diversity of experience. The poet turns his back on, sucking, and biting. He "transcends" these experiences and finds a meaning beyond them.

The woman participates in this unity only on the condition that she, too, turn away from these experiences, from the fragmentation and immediacy of the feminine, and accept his image.

The more we listen to the man's celebration of unity, the more it implies difference. This is not, moreover, the result of a particularly radical or feminist approach to the poem. There is something of Farwell's awareness in many of the poem's more conservative male critics. Wilbur Sanders points to this same issue in his discussion of the ambiguities of the last lines: "Whatever dies, was not mix'd equally; / If our two loves be one, or, thou and I / Love just alike in all, none of these loves can die" (ll. 19–21). The difficulty of maintaining this equality, he remarks, is "conditional upon impossible stabilities. . . . Almost certainly, though, the unresolved nature of the final stanza proceeds from the fact that, somewhere in the course of it, Donne loses the burning awareness of the woman's presence which makes the first two so potent; and he is left, consequently, with a lapful of doubts and misgivings, trying to piece them together into the required affirmation, and failing."[22]

Sanders's discussion suggests how difficult it is for the "imaginative unity of understanding"[23] between the couple to resist the effect of their differences. The man accepts and "understands" the woman only to lose his "burning" awareness of her person as he attempts to voice this understanding to her. He expresses not his feeling, the sincerity of his recognition, but the meaning of language as the suppression of the feminine. From this point of view, it is interesting to examine the similarities between the dramatic situations in "The Good-morrow" and "The Flea." In "The Good-morrow" the man and the woman wake together. He is speaking to her. The poem is not a simple description of their feelings for one another, composed from some omniscient point of view. Like the argument in "The Flea," it is a proposal which the man makes to the woman. He presents a certain reading of what has happened between them and asks her to accept this interpretation. In both the "masculine persuasive force" (Elegy XVI, l. 4) of the speaker is directed toward the silence of the woman; the speaker intends to elaborate this silence, to give the immediacy of the feminine a name.

It is true, of course, that in "The Good-morrow" this force ap-

pears as the effect of a particularly intense sincerity rather than
in the overtly coercive arguments of the speaker in "The Flea."
But, from this point of view, what seems important in the sincerity of the lover is less the way it expresses his feelings for her
than the way this intensity seems to insist on an acceptance no
less unconditional than the one demanded by the poet in "The
Flea." This lover presents his "true plain" (l. 16) heart in his face
and asks that it be responded to with an equal simplicity. His
message is an "I love you" which will accept only itself in return.
It will be answered only on its own terms. At this point the lover's statement loses its personal quality, which is absorbed in the
relentless power of language to define. So his expression of love
seems only another version of masculine assertiveness. "He wants
the same thing they all do," she might think. The woman would
have no choice but to react against this assertiveness and to insist
on her difference. They would begin to fight, to speak and enact
not their understanding of one another but rather the endless argument between men and women.

We can see the consistency and inevitability of this process if
we look again at "The Flea" and search for those moments when,
by the most generous interpretation possible, we might be able to
hear in the man's language the offer of a personal understanding.
In the last stanza, for example, he seems to acknowledge the
woman's power when he says "Just so much honor, when thou
yield'st to me, / Will waste, as this flea's death took life from
thee." (ll. 26–27) These lines are obviously intended to trivialize the woman's surrender in a way which will make it more likely.
They are clearly meant, in other words, to secure the mastery of
the woman. But it is also possible to read them against this overt
meaning and find in them at least the suggestion of a personal desire to accommodate her. Perhaps in trivializing the death of the
flea the poet is trivializing the "death" of his own images and of
his own power to define. Perhaps he is trying to detach himself
from an unquestioning acceptance of the masculine and to indi-
cate some recognition and understanding of its difference.

This reading is too ingenuous to be sincere, of course. It seems
exactly the kind of thing the man would want the woman to believe, a mock surrender which disguises his real intention. The
implications of his continuing self-assertion are more real than

any suggestion of effacement or surrender. But if we try to locate the elements in his discourse which privilege our suspicion,
we can see that the most important by far is the fact that the poet
explicitly voices his acknowledgment. The masculine creates itself by imposing its meaning on the silence of the feminine. The
poet may intend to acknowledge the power of this silence, but in
acknowledging it he speaks it, fixes it, gives the moment of orgasm and loss an image and a meaning, however trivial. The poet's accommodation of the feminine, by the very fact of its being
said, becomes the next stage in the masculine attempt to seduce
and define femininity.

However ridiculous this reading of the poet's intention might
seem, it does suggest the real difficulties in attempting to talk to
another across the arbitrary differences which separate us. It is
always easy to express this desire for an equality of understanding. In situations such as these, however, it is not how words are
intended which determines their meaning, but the way they are
understood. And our resistance to hearing anything but mastery
in the man's voice or disruption in the woman's gesture alerts us
to the way hearing is a slave to these differences.

The persistence of difference is one way of explaining the nervous quality of the *Songs and Sonnets*. In both "The Flea" and
"The Good-morrow" seduction is essentially an attempt to escape difference, to solicit or force a response which is equal to
the seducer's desire, which will correspond to this desire and
complete it. But the failure of the poet's mastery or the lover's
sincere wish to find this moment of "centric happiness" ("Loves
Alchemy," l. 2), when desire finds its own reflection and closes
on itself, means that seducers will always be in a distanced relation with the object of their desire. Rather than forming a narrative in which the man moves from the aggression of "The Flea"
toward perfect symmetry of satisfaction in "The Good-morrow,"
the *Songs and Sonnets* record a more broken rhythm in which he
is continually returned to this situation of difference and frustration.

In concrete terms, Donne's lovers will always argue. The dream
of satisfaction is a dream of the perfect response. It is a vision of
a listener who comprehends your intention completely and returns it to you as the affirmation of understanding. But the inevi-

tability of difference means that the seducer will never be completely understood because he will never be heard clearly. The
frustration of the lover is that of never being able to make the
other see the obviousness and specificity of his or her own intention. As soon as this intention is stated or expressed, it is interpreted by the other in its most conventional meaning. As a result,
they live in the continual frustration of this difference between
what they mean and what the other hears and understands.

This is an argument from which it is possible to withdraw but
never to conclude. It seems to offer only the stereotyped opposition between man and woman or the retreat into silence and solitude. But if this is true, it is certainly not all. Even in "The Flea,"
where the man and the woman do enact these stereotyped roles
so clearly, there is something more. There is no sense of closure
at the conclusion of this poem. The poet transforms the death of
the flea as an image of the loss of orgasm, recuperates the negative
effect of the woman's gesture, and makes it a positive moment in
the man's seduction. But this metaphor is certainly no less subject
to another disruption. Yet if there is no sense of closure, there is
no sense of the growing rage at this perpetual frustration. We
could imagine this argument continuing indefinitely by choice.

In the persistence of the man and the woman in "The Flea," a
persistence which continues in spite of frustration, we can see another and, in some ways, more interesting form of address. The
latter localizes desire in the other as *other*, as that which is beyond assimilation or understanding and which addresses this other
across the difference which separates them. Such a conversation,
of course, could never become the basis of an understanding
which unites the participants. Its form would always be the
form of an argument in which the other would be addressed as
resistance, as that which will always be alien because it will never
reflect or understand the subject and return the subject to itself
as a clear and explicit meaning. But this other can still be addressed personally, even though his or her response will never coincide with this personal message. Each can vary the connotations
of speaking and acting, elaborate them in ways that cannot change
their explicit meaning but that can make this meaning the vehicle
of a personal intonation. In this way the man and the woman
could appropriate the argument, make its inevitability the form of

a personal conversation, although, again, this conversation could never be anything but an argument. Their exchange would only be one of suggestion and connotation which could never be read clearly or in such a way that their difference could be resolved.

To put this another way, we can see that Donne's poem is not just the articulation and enactment of this stereotyped opposition between masculine and feminine. If it were, it would be easy to imagine any given couple in their situation. But this is not possible, even with great effort. There is a specificity to their exchange which makes "The Flea" attractive and amusing instead of merely contentious.

The specificity of the man's address to the woman obviously lies in the witty development of his argument, his elaboration of the image of the flea as one of sexual union, a marriage temple, the "death" of orgasm. If we read these images as the direct expression of the poet's desire of mastery, then they seem simply a lavish celebration of his assumption of this power. But if we think of "The Flea" as a conversation occurring beyond the poet's demystification and acceptance of difference, then this luxury of statement takes on another connotation. The very excess of the comparison appears to be a way of delaying the inevitability of this final meaning. The elaborateness of the poet's style seems to result from the effort he makes to divert the imperative of language to define and make explicit. In this delay, the poet addresses the woman and indicates his recognition of her as other. But because the suggestion of this delay is always subject to the completion of the sentence and to the desire of language itself to define and master, it is a message that will never be anything more than a contradictory suggestion. He will never be able to make it explicit, for as long as he states his desire, the latter will finally be defined by the conditions of language itself. The explicitness of language will always be understood by the woman as mastery.

The poet, then, speaks indirectly in the diversion and delay of this final meaning. But the woman, we notice, pauses as well. At the opening of the second stanza she waits, defers her gesture, in order to allow the man time to react and speak. This might sound trivial, but it is not. The poem would not exist if she had not waited, and we could not imagine the speaker of the poem interested in a woman who would not respond to his wit by waiting. Her pause delays the gesture, postpones the disruptive expression of the feminine in the same way that the conceits of the poet delay the expression of the masculine. Her pause is what particularizes her action and makes it a response to the speaker—the recognition and acceptance of his desire—rather than merely the rejection of the masculine by the feminine.

In a way, then, the man and the woman do speak to one another. Their conversation takes place on this level of connotation and suggestion which results from the way they vary their articulation and enactment of determined and opposing meanings. They speak to each other to the extent that their pauses and deferrals allow them to vary the rhythm of their performance and make this performance a kind of conversation.

The messages transmitted in such a conversation are transitory, contingent, and excessive in the sense of not finally necessary to the "real" meaning of the statement; they are therefore not conclusive in the sense of determining this meaning. To assign personal expression to these qualities is to assimilate it to several categories: sentimentality, of course; irony as that which plays off of and exceeds the explicit; diversion; and minor errors in style and spelling which personalize a statement but do not define its content. This should remind not only the critic, who has tried to hear these personal rhythms in the language of a poem, but anyone who has tried, across some difference, to read them in the language of another that it is just these occasional communications which are easiest to miss, hardest to interpret and analyze, and, of course, the most incompatible with publication.

SEDUCTIONS CAN TAKE MANY FORMS and directions. But, not surprisingly, the seductions in the works which follow are all generated by the same argument between masculine and feminine which serves as the structural principle behind "The Flea." In the initial movement of this argument, as we have seen, the couple attempts to withdraw from the surveillance of convention in order to confront one another directly. Pornography in general, and *Fanny Hill* in particular, offer an interesting version of this initial situation. In Cleland's novel the opposition between definition and interruption provides one way of understanding Fanny's story. But this argument is also played out between the work and its readers, an encounter which, after *Fanny Hill* was censored, also takes place surreptitiously, in some private corner. Here Fanny's narrative continuously attempts to seduce her readers, disturb their voyeuristic mastery, and assimilate them to the terms of her own experience.

# II

# Fanny Hill *and*

# the Androgynous Reader

ANYONE WHO ATTEMPTS TO WRITE a scholarly essay on John Cleland's *Fanny Hill* is immediately confronted with a certain ambivalence. On the one hand, it is clearly a significant, if not crucial, text in literary and intellectual history, having obvious relations with the familiar letter, spiritual autobiography, rogue literature and, through these, with the "origin" of the novel. On the other hand, by both past as well as present standards, *Fanny Hill* is a pornographic novel. In their book *Pornography and the Law* Drs. Eberhard and Phyllis Kronhausen list eleven characteristics of hard-core pornography: seduction, where the victim is a willing collaborator; defloration; incest; permissive-seductive parent figure; profaning the sacred; "dirty" words; supersexed males; nymphomaniac females; Negroes and Asiatics as sex symbols; homosexuality; and flagellation.[1] If we substitute Dick, the idiot boy Louisa seduces in Part II, for Negroes and Asiatics and allow for Cleland's intentional de-emphasis of the more transgressive aspects of sexuality, it is clear that his novel falls well within these boundaries.

But to say that a novel is pornographic implies more than that it describes certain activities. It implies that it describes them in a certain way. This is particularly clear if we juxtapose *Fanny Hill* with *Moll Flanders*. In many ways these two narratives are one and the same novel. They are memoirs of young girls who are seduced, through a combination of necessity and inclination, pass through a series of adventures, repent, and marry their true loves. In both there is a persistent emphasis on sexuality. From a certain point of view it is possible to raise the classic issues of Defoe's work—the irony of the text; the conflict between religious patterns in the spiritual autobiography with patterns of economic determinism—using Cleland's novel.[2]

The contemplative reader who seeks an issue to understand and analyze, then, will come away from both novels equally satisfied. But the reader who reads in order to experience desire probably will leave *Moll Flanders* before her story is finished. Defoe's novel is, of course, a remarkably unsensual work. While Defoe sometimes takes note of Moll's sexual pleasure, he never lingers over it. But this only emphasizes the way in which *Fanny Hill*, in its attention to Fanny's physical pleasure, solicits the reader's pleasure as well. Depending on circumstances, of course, most if not all books can be read for pleasure, even sexual pleasure. But pornography obviously intends to establish this relationship with a particular intensity.

As a work of pornography, *Fanny Hill* attempts to seduce its readers in a direct and physical way. The novel wants to arouse the reader, and the more it succeeds, the more intense the reader's desire becomes, the more it denies the detached passivity of contemplation and demands action. Consequently, the reader who is seduced by this novel, who responds to it in this way, is inevitably driven to another activity. In his contribution to *Does Pornography Matter?* Geoffrey Gorer defines the position of this reader in a matter-of-fact but accurate way: "The object of pornography is hallucination. The reader is meant to identify either with the narrator (the 'I' character) or with the general situation to a sufficient extent to produce at least the physical concomitants of sexual excitement; if the work is successful, it should produce orgasm."[3] The desiring reader, then, is not one who studies a text but one who is enticed by it, who allows himself to be manipulated by it and, finally, who makes love to it. To write about *Fanny Hill* as pornography is, inevitably, to write about the reader's excitement and orgasm, since his masturbation is as much the "logical" expression of this kind of reading as the scholarly essay is the "logical" expression of a contemplative analysis.[4]

Most of the scholarly literature on *Fanny Hill* has focused on

the apparent imbalance in Cleland's work between these two readings of the text. This is particularly true of those articles which
were written more or less directly in response to questions of the
novel's "seriousness" and "merit" raised by the government in an
attempt to prevent its distribution in 1963. These readings either
tend to suppress the erotic elements in order to privilege the
novel's thematic coherence or to accept its pornographic effect
but lament the resulting lack of unity.[5]

This ambivalence becomes a more interesting issue, however,
if we temporarily leave aside the question of "unity" and simply
focus attention on the way *Fanny Hill*—like any pornographic
work which includes almost equal parts of erotic description and
novelistic exposition—presents itself to the reader as a version of
the paradox of the erotic theme.[6] Because it offers readers a narration which embodies a meaning, it makes available to them the
role of interpreter. They survey the body of the text, master it,
define it and, as a result of this process, articulate a coherent
image of themselves. But this pursuit of meaning, of course, leads
them to ponder other places as well. Reading, at this point, becomes the agency of a more immediate physical experience. They
find their concentration wandering and their attention focused
elsewhere. If they surrender to this experience, they fall into dissolution. They not only lose their vision of the novel's coherence
but of their own coherence as well.[7]

Of course, any discussion of the radical effect of pornography
has to be carefully qualified. Most of the current commentary on
pornographic works is concerned with showing how they not
only reflect but reinforce the ideological structure of a society in
which men are given the power to oppress women.[8] From this
point of view, the pleasures of pornography no more constitute
a radical attack on the ultimate coherence of the masculine prerogative than an executive's interlude with a call girl constitutes
a threat to big business. The reader, like the executive, simply
uses Fanny the way men have always used women. He pays for
her, takes her at his leisure, opens her where he will, and discards
her when he is tired of her.[9] The disruption of sexuality, no matter how intense, is immediately recuperated as the sign of the
man's mastery over the woman. The descriptions of "Fanny's"
pleasure serve only to reflect and intensify this stereotyped male

position of dominance, to naturalize this ideology and make it seem a part of woman's own "natural" desire, too.

It is understandable why some feminist critics would focus on those aspects of Cleland's novel which reflect conventional ideology. The novel, after all, does preserve the traditional opposition between masculine and feminine. It does not displace the relationship between a man and a woman to some area of the "erotic" which lies outside issues of mastery, domination, and surrender. But it would be a mistake to move too quickly from this fact to a narrow and conservative reading of *Fanny Hill*. Such a reading, strangely, has the effect of reinforcing these conventional structures by assuming that within the opposition masculine/feminine a man's desire will *always* be to master and a woman's to surrender, so that any individual fantasy provoked by the work will immediately correspond to the political structure which determines the traditional difference between the sexes.

But this is not necessarily so clear. Writing on pornography in general, Diana George attacks an unquestioning feminist rejection of this literature. (By pornography, again, George means works which center the relationship between men and women around the issues of mastery and submission.) Her essay is written against any attempt to create an "innocent" realm of the erotic by divesting sexuality of all its violent components. George's argument is complex, but one important element in it is her assertion that the effort to simplify sexuality in this way denies the "inner conflict in the sexuality of both sexes,"[10] denies, in other words, the masculine aspect of any woman and the feminine component of any man. On this basis George defends pornographic images of rape and violence (defends them as *images*, not as acts) because they testify to real, if unconscious, desires which must be recognized and dealt with.

But for George these unconscious desires are not simply feminine desires of submission. While she says that she must acknowledge a part of her that wants to be the subject of acts of violent sexuality ("I want to be killed"), she must also acknowledge another part of her that wants to direct such actions toward others ("I want to kill you"). She concludes, "I can muffle that [latter] voice, but not destroy it by denying it."[11] One of the effects of pornography, in other words, is the way it discloses a masculine desire for domination within the woman. But, clearly, a novel which awakens such a fantasy also works against an ideology which assigns her an exclusively feminine experience.

By the same token, the radical aspect of *Fanny Hill* appears in the way it provokes a feminine desire in the male reader. No less than Donne's "The Flea," the rhythm of Cleland's novel involves the interruption of a project of mastery and definition by an effect which not only dissipates but seduces. The intensity and disruption of the man's sexual experience, in other words, is not immediately recuperated as the sign of his power over the woman. It is lived for itself. In this way "Fanny" becomes the locus *not* of a conception of female sexuality but of the kind of feminine sexuality which is available to the man. This is a pleasure which avoids recuperation and, for that reason, allows him to escape the tedious responsibility of definition and mastery which society has imposed upon him. Cleland is interested in investigating the kind of freedom which this pleasure seems to afford. But he is also interested in the way this pleasure elicits a sense of internal play between masculine and feminine which subverts conventional gender identifications. In this way the novel moves toward a certain idea of androgyny in which the equality between masculine and feminine triumphs over the difference between the sexes and allows the man and the woman to converse freely across this difference.

With this in mind, we might look closely at one incident which takes place early in the novel.[12] It occurs during Fanny's stay at Mrs. Brown's, immediately after her arrival in London. As a part of Mrs. Brown's scheme to corrupt the still innocent Fanny, the maid, Phoebe, takes her to a room from which they can observe an afternoon meeting between Polly, another of Mrs. Brown's whores, and her lover. The passage is long but worth quoting in its entirety. It embodies everything that is ambiguous in a reader's relation to any text which is at once thematic and pornographic. But it also shows us exactly how *Fanny Hill* formulates this ambivalence, how the novel defines these positions for its readers and how it plays one off against the other.

The young gentleman was the first person I saw, with his back directly towards me, looking at a print. Polly was not yet come:

in less than a minute tho', the door opened, and she came in; and at the noise the door made he turned about, and came to meet her, with an air of the greatest tenderness and satisfaction.

After saluting her, he led her to a couch that fronted us, where they both sat down, and the young Genoese help'd her to a glass of wine, with some Naples bisket on a salver.

Presently, when they had exchanged a few kisses, and questions in broken English on one side, he began to unbutton, and, in fine, stript to his shirt.

As if this had been the signal agreed on for pulling off all their cloaths, a scheme which the heat of the season perfectly favoured, Polly began to draw her pins, and as she had no stays to unlace, she was in a trice, with her gallant's officious assistance, undress'd to all but her shift.

When he saw this, his breeches were immediately loosen'd, waist and knee bands, and slipped over his ankles, clean off; his shirt collar was unbuttoned too then, first giving Polly an encouraging kiss, he stole, as it were, the shift off the girl, who being, I suppose, broke and familiariz'd to this humour, blush'd indeed, but less than I did at the apparition of her, now standing stark-naked, just as she came out of the hands of pure nature, with her black hair loose and a-float down her dazzling white neck and shoulders, whilst the deepen'd carnation of her cheeks went off gradually into the hue of glaz'd snow: for such were the blended tints and polish of her skin.

This girl could not be above eighteen: her face regular and sweet-featur'd, her shape exquisite; nor could I help envying her two ripe enchanting breasts, finely plump'd out in flesh, but withal so round, so firm, that they sustain'd themselves, in scorn of any stay: then their nipples, pointing different ways, mark'd their pleasing separation; beneath them lay the delicious tract of the belly, which terminated in a parting or rift scarce discernible, that modestly seem'd to retire downwards, and seek shelter between two plump fleshy thighs: the curling hair that overspread its delightful front, cloathed it with the richest sable fur in the universe: in short, she was evidently a subject for the painters to court her sitting to them for a pattern of female beauty, in all the true pride and pomp of nakedness.

The young Italian (still in his shirt) stood gazing and transported at the sight of beauties that might have fir'd a dying hermit; his eager eyes devour'd her, as she shifted attitudes at his discretion: neither were his hands excluded their share of the high feast, but wander'd, on the hunt of pleasure, over every part and inch of her body, so qualified to afford the most exquisite sense of it.

In the mean time, one could not help observing the swell of his shirt before, that bolster'd out, and shewed the condition of things behind the curtain: but he soon remov'd it, by slipping his shirt over his head; and now, as to nakedness, they had nothing to reproach one another.

The young gentleman, by Phoebe's guess, was about two and twenty; tall and well limb'd. His body was finely form'd, and of a most vigorous make, square-shoulder'd, and broad-chested: his face was not remarkable in any way, but for a nose inclining to the Roman, eyes large, black, and sparkling, and a ruddiness in his cheeks that was the more a grace, for his complexion was of the brownest, not of that dusky dun colour which excludes the idea of freshness, but of that clear, olive gloss which, glowing with life, dazzles perhaps less than fairness, and yet pleases more, when it pleases at all. His hair, being too short to tie, fell no lower than his neck, in short easy curls; and he had a few sprigs about his paps, that garnish'd his chest in a style of strength and manliness. Then his grand movement, which seem'd to rise out of a thicket of curling hair that spread from the root all round thighs and belly up to the navel, stood stiff and upright, but of a size to frighten me, by sympathy, for the small tender part which was the object of its fury, and which now lay expos'd to my fairest view; for he had, immediately on stripping off his shirt, gently push'd her down on the couch, which stood conveniently to break her willing fall. Her thighs were spread out to their utmost extension, and discovered between them the mark of the sex, the red-center'd cleft of flesh, whose lips, vermilioning inwards, ex-prest a small rubid line in sweet miniature, such as *Guido's* touch of colouring could never attain to the life or delicacy of.

Phoebe, at this, gave me a gentle jog, to prepare me for a whispered question: whether I thought my little maidenhead was much less? But my attention was too much engross'd, too much enwrapp'd with all I saw, to be able to give her any answer.

By this time the young gentleman had changed her posture from lying breadth to length-wise on the couch; but her thighs were still spread, and the mark lay fair for him, who now kneeling between them, display'd to us a side-view of that fierce erect machine of his, which threaten'd no less than splitting the tender victim, who lay smiling at the uplifted stroke, nor seem'd to decline it. He looked upon his weapon himself with some pleasure, and guiding it with his hand to the inviting slit, drew aside the lips, and lodg'd it (after some thrusts, which Polly seem'd even to assist) about half way; but there it stuck, I suppose from its growing thickness: he draws it again, and just wetting it with spittle, re-enters, and with ease sheath'd it now up to the hilt, at which Polly gave a deep sigh, which was quite another tone than one of pain; he thrusts, she heaves, at first gently, and in a regular cadence; but presently the transport began to be too violent to observe any order or measure; their motions were too rapid, their kisses too fierce and fervent for nature to support such fury long: both seem'd to me out of themselves; their eyes darted fires: "Oh! . . . oh! . . . I can't bear it . . . It is too much . . . I die . . . I am going . . ." were Polly's expressions of extasy: his joys were more silent; but soon broken murmurs, sighs heart-fetch'd, and at length a dispatching thrust, as if he would have forced himself up her body, and then motionless languor of all his limbs, all shewed that the die-away moment was come upon him; which she gave signs of joining with, by the wild throwing of her hands about, closing her eyes, and giving a deep sob, in which she seemed to expire in an agony of bliss.

When he had finish'd his stroke, and got from off her, she lay still without the least motion, breathless, as it should seem, with pleasure. He replaced her again breadth-wise on the couch, unable to sit up, with her thighs open, between which I could observe a kind of white liquid, like froth, hanging about the outward lips of that recently opened wound, which now glowed with a deeper red. Presently she gets up, and throwing her arms round him, seemed far from undelighted with the trial he had put her to, to judge at least by the fondness with which she ey'd and hung upon him.

For my part, I will not pretend to describe what I felt all over me during this scene; but from that instant, adieu all fears of what man could do unto me; they were now changed into such ardent desires, such ungovernable longings, that I could have pull'd the first of that sex that should present himself, by the sleeve, and offered him the bauble, which I now imagined the loss of would be a gain I could not too soon procure myself.

Phoebe, who had more experience, and to whom such sights were not so new, could not however be unmoved at so warm a scene; and drawing me away softly from the peep-hole, for fear of being over-heard, guided me as near the door as possible, all passive and obedient to her least signals.

Here was no room either to sit or lie, but making me stand with my back towards the door, she lifted up my petticoats, and with her busy fingers fell to visit and explore that part of me where now the heat and irritations were so violent that I was perfectly sick and ready to die with desire; that the bare touch of her finger, in that critical place, had the effect of a fire to a train, and her hand instantly made her sensible to what a pitch I was wound up, and melted by the sight she had thus procured me. Satisfied then with her success in allaying a heat that would have made me impatient of seeing the continuation of the transactions between our amourous couple, she brought me again to the crevice so favourable to our curiosity. (pp. 33–39)

*Fanny Hill,* obviously, is a first-person narration. Readers see events through her eyes and their reactions will be, in some way, a function of hers. Given this fact, what can we say about the way vision structures Fanny's desire during this interlude?

First, it is clear that this relation between wanting and seeing is not a simple one. It has two distinct aspects. On the one hand, vision completes desire, shows desire its "true" nature and end. Initially Fanny experiences sexual excitement as the effect of "an inflammable principle of pleasure" (p. 28), an "itch of florid warm-spirited blood" (p. 29). It appears, in other words, as the particular sensitivity associated with physical irritation or the heightened sensitivity which announces a physical need such as hunger or thirst. This need is encouraged, of course, both by Phoebe's touches during the first night Fanny spends at Mrs. Brown's and by the conversations of the other girls. But, despite this, it still remains essentially blind, uninformed about itself and the nature of the satisfaction it demands. In Cleland's novel neither touch nor the spoken word is adequate to educate Fanny, to explicate the nature of this satisfaction. She must be shown. Although sexuality begins in the immediacy of sensation, the heightened sensitivity of an area that is inflamed or itches, it must displace itself from this immediacy and pass through vision before it can be fully educated.[13]

From this point of view, an obvious meaning behind this scene and the similar one which precedes it—in which Fanny observes the meeting between the grenadier and the older woman—lies in the way both scenes respond to her need to see. One aspect of Cleland's novel implies the "natural" complementarity of men and women. In witnessing the first encounter, Fanny's gaze is drawn inevitably to the man's erection. But, she tells us, "I soon had my eyes called off by a more striking object, that entirely engross'd them. Her sturdy stallion had now unbutton'd, and produced naked, stiff, and erect, that wonderful machine, which I had never seen before, and which, for the interest my own seat of pleasure began to take furiously in it, I star'd at with all the eyes I had" (p. 30). Faced with this spectacle, Fanny's eyes solve the problem posed by her desire. The instinctive nature of this discovery and the unconscious reaction of her "seat of pleasure" (p. 30) naturalize this relationship and make it seem part of the inevitable order of things.[14]

The interlude between Polly and her lover, in turn, simply completes Fanny's education in the natural progression of sexuality. When she returns to her room after witnessing this encounter, she finds her feelings organized, given a referent. "I laid me down on the bed," she writes, "stretched myself out, joining and ardently wishing, and requiring any means to divert my desires, which all pointed strongly to their pole; man" (p. 33). But Fanny is still inhibited by what seems to her the inexplicable and unnatural size of the man in relation to her own small stature. For this reason Phoebe organizes the second spectacle around Polly, who is more Fanny's equal in age and build. When Fanny witnesses Polly's satisfaction, her own uneasiness is stilled. "For my part," she writes, "I will not pretend to describe what I felt all over me during this scene; but from that instant, adieu all fears of what man could do unto me; they were now changed into such ardent desires . . ." (p. 38).

This second scene, then, leaves Fanny ready for "more solid food" (p. 41). When she returns to her bedroom with Phoebe, she now finds her companion a less than adequate substitute. "She takes hold of my hand," Fanny tells us, "and . . . forced it half strivingly towards those parts, where, now grown more knowing, I missed the main object of my wishes; and finding not even the shadow of what I wanted, where everything was so flat, or so hollow" (p. 41). Fanny's education here involves the fixation of her desire on a single object, with her pleasure dependent on the actual presence or absence of this object. This condensation and focusing of desire prepares Fanny for her first glimpse of Charles the next morning, and this encounter, in turn, generates the plot of the novel: the narrative of her discovery, loss, and rediscovery of the object of her love.

But there is, obviously, more to Fanny's experience here than her discovery of the natural object of desire. Her viewing gives her access to a pleasure which not only is free of the actual presence of the object but which, finally leads her to turn away from the sight of it. This aspect of erotic vision does not merely lead desire to its object but directs pleasure away from the object, diverts it in a way that gives viewing a particularly independent status. Although, for example, the "interest" (p. 30) her "seat of pleasure" (p. 30) takes in the grenadier's "wonderful machine" (p. 30) does alert her to the object in the world that seems "naturally" to answer her desire, this desire has a more immediate expression. The sight and sound of the lovers, Fanny writes, "thrill'd to the very soul of me, and made every vein of my body circulate liquid fires: the emotion grew so violent that it almost intercepted my respiration" (p. 31). Under the pressure of this intensity, Fanny takes the only possible action. "I twisted my thighs," she continues, "squeezed, and compressed the lips of that virgin slit, and following mechanically the example of Phoebe's manual operation of it, as far as I could find admission, brought on at last the critical extasy, the melting flow, into which nature, spent with excess of pleasure, dissolves and dies away" (p. 31). In a similar way, Fanny's initial encounter with Phoebe leads to a dream "the transports of which are scarce inferior to those of waking real action" (p. 17). And here she is so "melted by the sight" (p. 39) of Polly and her lover that she allows herself to be manipulated by Phoebe's "busy fingers" (p. 39).

The emphasis in these moments is obviously not on vision as an instrumentality which leads the subject into the world toward a determined object of desire. Instead, vision is an erotic experience which generates an intensity in and of itself, an intensity which Fanny's descriptions suggest is "scarce inferior" to "real action" (p. 17). Erotic spectacle diverts sexuality from the pursuit of its natural object and frees it from the necessity of this object's real presence. It is enough here that Fanny see these couples making love. She is not driven to enter the scene herself. It remains simply spectacle. What is important is the intensity of desire and pleasure, and for this the spectacle itself is sufficient. The situation exists to produce this pleasure and, by the same token, any situation which would produce this intensity would be desirable. Pleasure here is not bound in a fixed relation to a single object or situation.

This attention to the diverting pleasure of erotic viewing has been one important element in Fanny's education at Mrs. Brown's. If we think for a moment about the way her education has been staged dramatically in the early pages of the novel, we can see that Cleland does not emphasize a simple relation among vision, desire, and its object. Fanny is not driven to enter this scene between Polly and her lover, nor does she attempt to seduce Charles when she sees him for the first time. In other words, vision does not provoke Fanny to act in an immediate and direct way that would emphasize a simple, "natural" relationship between sexuality and vision. Fanny's desire is consummated only after a protracted series of "scenes": the "luscious" (p. 17) dream she has the first night with Phoebe and the two spectacles she and Phoebe observe together. In these instances vision finds its own pleasure. In fact, almost all of the characters in *Fanny Hill* indulge in a passion for viewing which is independent of natural sexuality. Sometimes these moments are used simply to supplement this natural movement of desire. During their first night together Phoebe pauses to uncover Fanny because, in her words, "my sight must be feasted as well as my touch . . . I must devour with my eyes" (p. 16). The Genoese merchant, after the fashion of his country, undresses Polly completely and lingers over the sight. Even when he is on the point of entering her, he stops for a moment and "looks upon his weapon himself with some pleasure" (p. 37). But *Fanny Hill* also emphasizes the joys of erotic viewing in and of itself. At least half the sexual encounters in the book take place in front of someone: Fanny's initiation; Louisa's seduction of Dick. Mrs. Cole, in fact, observes from her closet all the scenes which take place at her establishment. In this novel sexuality is staged in such a way that the pleasure of watching is an important moment.

Fanny discovers the true nature of her desire only when she is captured by Mrs. Brown and finds herself manipulated according to the schemes of Mrs. Brown and Phoebe. It is here she learns that man is the pole toward which this desire points and it is here that she meets Charles. But in the course of this she also discovers another pleasure. Because Mrs. Brown's plot requires that Fanny be excited to the point that she will accept any man who purchases her maidenhead, the natural expression of her sexuality is momentarily suspended. It is diverted by the layout of Mrs. Brown's house, with its voyeuristic maze of closets and peepholes, in a way that uncovers a level of erotic viewing where vision is not simply that agency through which desire recognizes its natural complement but is a source of pleasure in and of itself.

It is not possible, of course, to talk about the ambivalence of Fanny's desire without recognizing its similarity to the ambiguous position of the novel's reader. This similarity would be most obvious in the case of readers as innocent as Fanny herself, readers who would be drawn to the book, as Fanny is drawn to the spectacle of Polly and her lover, by a desire to learn the true nature and object of their desire. But it would also apply to a certain kind of scholarly reader who is characterized by the "innocence" of the detached, contemplative point of view. Both of these would approach the book as an object of study, a source of knowledge. Its reading would be a means to an end, a way to gather essential information which would illuminate the real world. But once these two types of readers enter the world of the book, they find themselves seduced by a series of erotic spectacles which, however much they might inform, also serve to divert their desire from its "real" object. Like Fanny, they find themselves the innocent participants in shady dealings, in this case the commercial circulation of images of sexuality, which is pornography.

This assumes, of course, that the reader is seduced. It is certainly possible to read *Fanny Hill* without being aroused. But if, admitting this, we still allow the book its intention to seduce innocence, we can see that these readers will find their desire diverted, displaced into the experience of reading as a kind of erotic viewing. In this context these early incidents, with their emphasis on spectacle and masturbation, seem almost to function as a set of instructions intended for those who are unfamiliar with the use of pornographic texts.

Fanny's experience in this scene, then, is an example of the way the novel attempts to seduce the reader and structure his or her experience by making a particularly intense appeal to the visual.

The intensity of this appeal frees pleasure from its necessary relation to the real world; it allows the reader to reach orgasm without the actual presence of any object which is the natural complement of desire. *Fanny Hill*, in this scene, is an example of the way any fantasy, but particularly any literature of fantasy, uses representation as a way of supplementing the "natural" so that the reader has access to sensations outside the limits of the "actual."[15]

As soon as we interpret the duality of Fanny's, and the reader's, position in this scene as the difference between a viewing which leads the subject to the mastery and possession of an object in the world—Fanny's discovery of Charles, for example—and one which leads the subject to be absorbed by the spectacle itself, we can see that this tension between active and passive corresponds to another, related opposition: the difference between masculine and feminine. At the opening of this scene Fanny enjoys the prerogatives of the detached voyeur for whom the sensibilities of the observed are literally an open book while her own privacy and control remain intact. The emphasis in the opening paragraphs of her description is on the scene within the room rather than her own reactions. She only refers to her own feelings at the end of the couple's first interlude together, and then only indirectly.

Here, for a moment at least, it would be difficult to separate the reader's perspective from Fanny's. The novel obviously offers the reader a similar voyeuristic position. *Fanny Hill* presents itself as a privileged communication: two confessional letters written by Fanny to an intimate confidant. The readers who buy the novel gain access to this communication and, through it, to Fanny's most intimate experiences and reactions. They own her, know her, use her. She must submit passively to their gaze. In this scene Fanny briefly escapes this position and moves from the observed to the observer. She views the scene within the room the way the reader "views" the scenes in the book.

Initially, then, this spectacle suggests that the novel offers the pleasure of viewing as a form of possession and control. The inquiring glance—either the innocent look of the naive reader or the detached one of the scholar—approaches this description in the same way Fanny approaches this scene, namely, with an unfocused desire for knowledge. Once these two types of readers are presented with this spectacle, however, both find this detached desire eroticized by the way their perspective defines it as a form of sexual power. This power, of course, traditionally belongs to the masculine, and the novel would seem to acknowledge this in the way Fanny first describes Polly. Polly is like "a subject for the painters to court her sitting to them for a pattern of female beauty, in all the true pride and pomp of nakedness. . . . the mark of the sex . . . vermilioning inwards, exprest a small rubid line in sweet miniature, such as *Guido's* touch of colouring could never attain to the life or delicacy of" (pp. 36–37). Here Fanny sees with the traditionally masculine eye which has determined that the feminine should be represented in Western art as an icon, an image of beauty for masculine contemplation.

This is the same perspective, of course, which Fanny offers the reader when, early in her narrative, she sketches an "unflatter'd picture" (p. 18) of herself, as well as the perspective enjoyed by Polly's lover as she "shifted attitudes at his discretion" (p. 36). The fact that Fanny assumes it, however briefly, makes it clear that in this novel the opposition between the masculine, which views, and the feminine, which is viewed, does not correspond to the fixed, biological difference between genders. They mark two opposed attitudes and experiences which are potentially available to both male and female characters.

This becomes clear, certainly, if we follow Fanny's reactions to the spectacle of Polly and her lover. Although she may have been seduced initially by the attractions of the masculine perspective, her final pleasure in this interlude is not presented as an extension or intensification of this point of view. The detachment of the voyeur emphasizes the difference between spectator and object. But when Fanny observes this scene, her experience does not develop in a way that asserts this difference. Polly blushes when she is first undressed, Fanny notes, adding that she blushed "less than I did at the apparition of her" (p. 36). When Polly's lover is about to enter her, Fanny notes that "his grand movement, which seem'd to rise out of a thicket of curling hair . . . stood stiff and upright, but of a size to frighten me, by sympathy, for the small tender part which was the object of its fury . . ." (p. 37).

In these moments Fanny discovers her anxiety reflected in Polly's situation. But she soon feels Polly's bliss as her own. This scene culminates, as will be recalled, with Fanny the unresisting subject of Phoebe's manipulations. She leads Fanny, "all passive and obedient," to the back of the closet, where "she lifted up my petticoats, and with her busy fingers fell to visit and explore that part of me where now the heat and irritations were so violent that I was perfectly sick . . ." (pp. 38–39). In submitting to Phoebe, Fanny repeats Polly's submission to the gaze and touch of her lover in a way that goes far beyond any sympathetic identification between two characters, or between a reader and a character. Fanny assumes the experience she has been watching, moves away from her vantage point, and recreates it in the center of her own detachment.

But at this point it is clear that Fanny's "masculine" perspective has been inverted. No longer the observer, she finds herself in the position of the one she has been observing. This inversion turns on the ambivalence of vision. On the one hand, vision implies distance and, therefore, detachment and control. But vision is also related in the novel to touch. Looking can be a "feast" (p. 36) because it has some of the sensory immediacy of taste. It can "melt and soften" (p. 21) because its effects can be felt on the skin like the sensation of heat. Consequently those who observes a scene of desire may find their position transformed. The one who watches someone touch becomes the one touched, the masculine observer becomes the feminine figure who is the subject of touch and observation.[16]

But, obviously, since both Fanny and the reader share the same perspective in this scene, whatever is true of one can also be true of the other; not, perhaps, of the reader who steadfastly contemplates the meaning of the book, but the reader who surrenders to this view, who becomes so "engross'd" (p. 37) and "enwrapp'd" (p. 37) by it that he is "melted by the sight" (p. 39) will find his own position inverted. Like Fanny, he turns from the spectacle and recreates in himself the scene he observes. In his surrender to the dissolving effects of sensation, he "becomes" Polly at the moment of her bliss. He, too, finds the masculine position of the voyeur feminized.[17]

The reader of *Fanny Hill*, the reader who allows himself to be seduced by the novel, will find himself in an ambivalent situation. He will be offered a position of detachment, control, perspective—the masculine position of the voyeur who commands his field of vision. But, if the book's seduction is successful, at some point the reader's relation to this scene will be transformed by the very intensity of the desire provoked by the visual spectacle it offers. At this point, rather than holding someone in his gaze he will find himself held by the sight. He will be touched by what he sees. The unity and apparent omnipotence of the one who watches will become the "passive" (p. 39) and disruptive experience of one who submits to and undergoes an experience. Finally vision itself will disappear in the dissolving moment of orgasm, in which Fanny writes, "every sense seemed lost . . ." (p. 88).

The interplay between difference which is established in this scene, the ease with which it moves both characters and readers between masculine and feminine attitudes, is one of the novel's most striking attributes. Since *Fanny Hill* makes the experience of masculine and feminine less a function of gender than of immediate relationship to others, the book has a strange quality of sexual ambivalence which distinguishes it from most pornography. Nevertheless, the development of Fanny's narrative can be described in terms of an opposition between two moments in which this ambivalence is determined, or resolved, in specific terms.

The first of these is a moment which privileges a masculine perspective. In this moment we see the object clearly, like a spectator before a painting. The clarity of our vision seems to confirm our omnipotence. The object subserviently submits to our gaze. It becomes an image of our power which attracts and fascinates us. The immediacy with which our look seems to possess this image returns us to ourselves as complete, definitive, and independent of the world beyond this horizon.

This moment of visual fascination occurs the morning after Fanny witnesses the scene between Polly and her lover. Rising early, she discovers Charles asleep in the parlor and is immediately enraptured by the sight of his beauty. "I command for ever," she writes, "the remembrance of thy first appearance to my ravish'd eyes" (p. 42). But this instant, which, according to Fanny, "con-

spir'd to fix my eyes and my heart" (p. 42), reaches its culmina-
tion when she and Charles wake after their first night together.

This scene is, again, characterized by the apparent freedom
with which the sexuality of Fanny and Charles seems to meta-
morphose in response to their situation. Again, Cleland initially
reverses the traditional relationship between lover and woman,
for it is Charles who sleeps and Fanny who looks. "Oh! could I
but paint his figure, as I see it now," she writes, "still present to
my transported imagination! A whole length of an all-perfect
manly beauty in full view. Think of a face without fault, glowing with all the opening bloom and vernal freshness of an age in
which beauty is of either sex, and which the first down over his
upper lip scarce began to distinguish" (pp. 52–53). Charles here
is a clearly androgynous figure. His beauty is "manly" but appropriate to "either sex." The passive subject of Fanny's gaze, he
becomes an image of feminine beauty. Fanny, in turn, becomes
masculine, aggressive. She pauses, "feasting my sight with all
those treasures of youthful beauty" until she has "devoured all
his naked charms with only two eyes" (p. 52).

It is Fanny who possesses and Charles who is possessed. But
when Charles awakens, it is only to assert what is "manly" (p. 52)
in his nature and return Fanny's gaze. "Presently," Fanny writes,
"as if he had proudly meant revenge for the survey I had smug-
gled of all his naked beauties, he spurns off the bed cloaths, and
trussing up my shift as high as it would go, too turns to feast his
eyes on all the gifts nature had bestow'd on my person" (p. 54).

Despite the fact that Fanny and Charles move from masculine
to feminine perspectives, there is no sense of an equality and
reciprocity between masculine and feminine experience. The
masculine gaze is not seduced or troubled in any way. It commands absolutely. Vision here is not a contemplative but an aggressive act which can "devour." The absolute power of vision
to appropriate its object defines the ambivalence of sexuality in
this encounter. The one who looks is masculine, whereas the one
who receives the look is feminine.

The primacy of the masculine explains the particular quality of
the sexuality in this interlude, the only one between Charles and
Fanny characterized by strong sadistic overtones. During the pre-

vious night, when Fanny loses "that darling treasure, that hidden mine, so eagerly sought after by the men, and which they never dig for but to destroy" (p. 41), she arrives "at excess of pleasure through excess of pain" (p. 51). In the passage which follows their awakening, Fanny's sex becomes a "wound" (p. 55) which takes Charles's "killing thrusts" (p. 55) until she is almost "suffocated" (p. 55) with pleasure. Again, there is no reciprocity here. Charles's sexuality is simply the extension of his vision; it appropriates without hesitation or opposition. Fanny, in turn, accepts his violence as the meaning of her experience and does not turn away from him in her moment of pleasure. Although this is a "joy inexpressible" (p. 55), it never loses its relation to his "killing thrusts" (p. 55). The otherness of the feminine is completely transformed and mastered. Her pleasure becomes simply an image, a celebration of Charles's masculine power.

At this moment Fanny exists only in relation to Charles, finding herself in him. The equality between them is like the mirroring relationship between a power and an effect which reflects and confirms the potency of its cause. Cleland's description here is an elaborate celebration of the phallic, and on this level, of course, Fanny is excluded from its performance. She can never extend her look to actual physical possession, as Charles does, and in this sense her femininity seems determined for her. Fanny's willing acceptance of her function as an image of male power in this scene marks one of the points where Cleland's novel seems most obviously a male fantasy. But it seems true, too, that the implications of this passage lie less in the way it confirms gender-determined sex roles than in the way Charles's sexuality here seems an extension and validation of the power of a certain way of looking which is open to either sex.

This interlude between Fanny and Charles defines the period between the former's escape from Mrs. Brown's and the latter's sudden disappearance. During this time they seem free from the life around them. Fanny will not have to prostitute herself; Charles is the favorite of his rich grandmother, whose generosity frees him from his father's rule. The conditions of their life reflect the apparent omnipotence of Charles's power. Their relationship seems as self-contained and hermetically sealed from the necessities and determining conditions of ordinary life as the relationship of Donne's lovers in their spherical world.

In the narrative of *Fanny Hill*, however, this moment is, in fact, only a moment. Charles and Fanny hardly become accustomed to one another when they are separated. Charles is kidnapped and sent to the South Seas on his father's orders in order to alienate him from his grandmother. Fanny is subjected to the schemes of their immoral and greedy landlady, Mrs. Jones. These intrusions are not, of course, merely accidental. From the first pages of the novel Cleland has presented Fanny's move from the country to London as both the result and the intensification of a visual mystification and bewilderment. Esther Davis, another girl from her village who moved to London and has returned for a visit, urges Fanny to come to the city by "piquing my childish curiosity with the fine sights which were to be seen in *London*" (p. 5). Fanny agrees to go partly as a result of the envy she and her friends feel when they "beheld Esther's scowered satin gowns, caps border'd with an inch of lace, taudry ribbons, and shoes belaced with silver" (p. 5).

When she arrives in London, moreover, she finds that "every sign or shop was a gazing-trap" (p. 9). She easily falls prey to Mrs. Brown, and it is Mrs. Brown, again, who schemes to make Fanny a whore by arranging the spectacle with Polly and her lover to inform and encourage Fanny's desire. From the beginning Fanny has been lead by her eyes. Charles seems only another "gazing-trap" destined to enmesh her even more deeply in a system in which every action and condition of her life will be determined by economic necessity. His disappearance reveals that the sense of immediate discovery and complete possession which vision affords is an illusion. The reality of Charles and Fanny's situation does not lie in the apparent self-sufficiency of the moment in which they contemplate and possess one another. Charles is not free to possess Fanny on his own terms. His meaning is spoken by a system of familial and economic interests of which he is unaware and over which he has little or no control.

In the same way, after his departure Fanny is not at liberty to keep herself for Charles's return. His disappearance leaves her in debt to Mrs. Jones and she finds herself, in the landlady's words, forced to abandon "your punctilio's and . . . make your market while you may" (p. 69). Fanny's actions become the mechanical expression of necessity. Mrs. Jones introduces her to Mr. H., who pays her debt and saves her from prison. In the face of this negotiation between her landlady/procuress and her new master, Fanny is powerless. When Mrs. Jones gives her a receipt for the debt Mr. H. has settled, she cannot even reach for it. Mr. H., she says, "forced me to secure it, by guiding my hand, which he had thrust it into, so as to make me passively put it into my pocket" (p. 70). She is not the agent of this exchange but its object.

The moment of visual fascination and sufficiency submits to more powerful and impersonal laws of economics. Initially Fanny can only experience her new situation as a complete alienation from her true desire for Charles. The first evening she spends with Mr. H. is, for her, joyless. During this interlude she is "without life or motion . . . innocent of the least sensation of pleasure" (p. 71). Like Moll Flanders, her surrender is the expression of necessity, not desire, and like much of Moll's narrative, sexuality here is reduced to exchange without sensuality.

This is not the case, however, in her second interlude with Mr. H. Pleasure enters this second encounter in a way that transforms her situation. Necessity, again, provides the occasion. But, under the influence of the wine and the mysterious aphrodisiacal effect of the "bridal posset" (p. 74), she discovers an ecstasy which is untouched by this necessity. Her enjoyment of this second interlude, she writes, is a result of "my animal spirits [which] rush'd mechanically to that center of attraction," so that she is "inly warmed, and stirr'd . . . beyond bearing" (p. 75). This is "a pleasure merely animal . . . struck out of the collision of the sexes by a passive bodily effect" (p. 75). Like the passivity of Fanny under Phoebe's "busy fingers" (p. 39), this moment is marked by a turning away from the spectacle of the world, the object, and a focusing of attention on the sensations of pleasure rather than their cause. These effects are "merely animal" (p. 75) and are not implicated or dependent on the dramatic particulars of the scene. "Any other man," Fanny writes, "would have been just the same to me" (p. 75).

This pleasure is one which has been freed from psychological and social constraints. It exists on the level of the "animal" (p. 75), where it is confirmed, finally, in the physiological effects of orgasm. But precisely because it seems to be "beyond" the normal economic and social considerations it provides Fanny not with a center but with an orientation which allows her to be active, to desire on her own terms, rather than simply to be the passive agent of economic or psychological necessity. For example, in her affair with H's servant, Will, Fanny is the aggressor, the seducer. And while the occasion for her action is a desire for revenge, this is not, finally, her motive. "As love never had, so now revenge had no longer any share in my commerce with this handsome youth," she writes. "The sole pleasures of enjoyment were now the link I held to him by" (p. 98).

This movement of desire toward the immediate experience of pleasure determines the incidental and episodic quality of Fanny's narrative during most of the second part of the novel, while she is living at Mrs. Cole's. Although technically Fanny is employed by Mrs. Cole, her life here is, in fact, an example of the independence of pleasure from the economic. Mrs. Cole, Fanny remarks, is characterized by "a rare alliance of pleasure with interest" (p. 107). But with the exception of Norbert, the rake to whom Fanny sells her phantom virginity, the terms of this alliance are such that economics never determines her actions. Money is simply the occasional result. Even when she accepts Mr. Bareville, the flagellant, it is from a "gust of fancy for trying a new experiment" (p. 166) rather than for the money he offers her.

Fanny's adventures at Mrs. Cole's are not determined by economic motives, nor do they express any other developing logic. She simply follows pleasure where it leads. The incidents involving Mr. Bareville, the man who is fixated on her hair, Louisa's seduction of Dick, and Emily's story of her evening at the masquerade ball do not even pretend to advance a plot. They exist simply to elicit a certain intensity of desire, and although the scene is necessary to produce this intensity, it will be left behind in the moment of pleasure. The succession of such moments, then, emphasizes the mobility of pleasure and the multiplicity of situations and objects which can generate it rather than its dependence on any one scene or object. None of these moments ever captures desire. Collectively they celebrate the "infinite diversity of tastes" (p. 166).

While she is at Mrs. Cole's, Fanny lives her desire according to the feminine principle. She turns away from the object, separates pleasure from its apparent cause, and liberates herself from the fixation of desire in the visual, which characterizes the masculine. By living her life for this pleasure, she remains free of the economy of her world at the very instant when she seems most determined by it. She infiltrates what is structured and finds her pleasure within this structure on her own terms. In this way she converts it to her own use. When pleasure is diffused in this way, it is unpredictable, uncontrollable, because it cannot be located by any necessary association with an image or object. Its occasion can be found anytime, anyplace. It comes and goes randomly. Fanny is never more independent, never more free, than when she is "working" for Mrs. Cole.

But to live for pleasure is to live for loss. "All pleasure," Fanny writes, tends "like life from its first instants, toward its own dissolution" (p. 211). The "delicious momentary dissolution" (p. 51) of orgasm, pursued relentlessly, leads to impotence and, finally, death. The condition of the young rake Norbert is a good example of this process. "At scare thirty," Fanny tells us, "he had already reduced his strength of appetite down to a wretched dependence on forc'd provocations, very little seconded by the natural power of a body jaded and racked off to the lees by constant repeated overdraughts of pleasure, which had done the work of sixty winters on his springs of life" (p. 153).

Norbert is saved from an early death only because he comes to love Fanny and discovers all his desires concentrated in her. Finding, she writes, "all that variety in me alone which he had sought for in a number of women, I . . . made him lose his taste for inconstancy, and new faces" (p. 164). Consequently, Fanny continues, "the love I had inspir'd him with bred a deference to me that was of great service to his health: for having by degrees . . . brought him to some husbandry of it, and to insure the duration of his pleasures by moderating their use . . . he was grown more delicate, more temperate, and in course more healthy" (p. 164). The only escape from the visual fixation of desire and the imprisoning determination which results from this fixation is to "follow pleasure where it leads" (p. 158). But it leads, evidently, to a dissolution whose only cure is the concentration of pleasure in one figure.


*Fanny Hill* NOT ONLY ESTABLISHES an ambivalence within its readers by encouraging their masculine selves to confront their feminine selves, it thematically expresses this ambivalence and considers the various possibilities of extending and living the alternatives which it defines. If we consider these alternatives from the point of view of a man such as the one in Donne's "The Flea," or from that of Charles, for example, when he meets Fanny in Mrs. Brown's and must choose a specific approach or form of address, we can see that up to this point in the novel his choices are at best only partially satisfying. Suppose, on the one hand, the man seduces the woman as Charles first seduces Fanny. Suppose he wins her by the forceful expression of his desire. In doing so Charles apparently saves Fanny from the determining effect of economic necessity which had led her there. In this he seems to have acted and spoken freely, outside of the values of money and class. He has realized his desire for her and chosen to be her lover rather than her customer. They seclude themselves and establish a domestic, private equality which is apparently independent of the world around them.

This apparent equality is obviously based on Charles's ability to free his personal voice from conventional masculine values, which would define Fanny in a completely stereotyped way. This allows him to talk to her freely and personally, to decide their relationship on his own terms. But if we look at the nature of their exchange at Mrs. Jones's, we see that, in fact, their conversation takes an immediately recognizable form and direction. Here Charles is the professor and Fanny the silent student who absorbs his every word. "In our cessations from active pleasure," Fanny writes, "Charles fram'd himself one, in instructing me . . . nor did I suffer one word to fall in vain from the mouth of my lovely teacher: I hung on every syllable he utter'd, and receiv'd, as oracles, all he said" (p. 63). What Charles does say, moreover, only reinforces the conventionality of their respective positions. He is teaching her the knowledge and manners appropriate to his station. He is equipping her to change her class, not to escape class structure altogether.

Charles seems to speak directly to Fanny and, in doing so, to appropriate the masculine power to define for his own desire. But the form and much of the content of his expression merely re-affirms the conventional values which this expression apparently sets itself against. In this he is not so much hypocritical as innocent and unaware of his inability to free the words he speaks from their social context, the broader conventional use of language, which ultimately determines their real effect. Charles means to say that he loves Fanny and will accept her as his equal. What he says, in fact, reduces her to a passive reflection of the values of his class and, ultimately, of the conventional masculine power to define the feminine. Once we see how his intention is lost in this larger intentionality of language, it comes as no surprise that their life at Mrs. Jones's is interrupted, and Charles's lessons superseded, by the greater voice of paternal and economic authority which dispatches Charles to the South Seas as his father's representative and returns Fanny to prostitution. This narrative movement simply enacts the real relationship between personal intention and conventional meaning in their earlier conversation.

Charles's experience here is the experience of any man who assumes that a certain masculine power whose basis lies in the conventional relationship between masculine and feminine is his to do with as he wishes. Like Charles, a man who naively identifies with this power so that he experiences it as a personal omnipotence will discover that in exercising it he has been doing convention's work and has inscribed at the center of his personal relationship with the woman he loves the structure of the world they both hope to escape. But suppose, on the other hand, that he surrenders to the feminine. Suppose he follows pleasure where it leads. In this way he is able to escape the masculine task of mastery and definition just as Fanny escapes the stereotype of her life as a prostitute, namely, by living these moments not as the expression of some imprisoning form of economic necessity but as the power of a feminine sexuality, or in the way readers escape the tyranny of the novel's theme during those moments when they turn away from the book to lose themselves in their own pleasure.

One of the most interesting aspects of Cleland's novel is the respect the author displays for these moments. They are not simply transgressive and do not depend for their intensity on a sense of their illicitness and outrageousness. More important, Cleland does not carry the intensity of these moments to the point of utter destruction, where the man will experience them as self-negation. They do fragment the unity of the masculine, but they do so in order to reveal specific pleasures which are positive, real, and independent.[18] Because of this, the man may ease into them, allow them to change his focus and open him up to experience. He does not have to struggle in order to recuperate the loss of pleasure as the sign of mastery because this loss is not pure loss. It is more a liberating transformation. The feminine is still opposed to the masculine for Cleland, but it is not hostile to the male. On the contrary, it allows him to transcend the narrow confines of traditional roles. Pleasure discovers beneath the abstractness of these roles an androgynous potential which provides access to both masculine and feminine experiences.[19]

Yet however real, immediate and liberating these pleasures may be, the man can never integrate them to make a unified whole. As the example of Norbert makes clear, his life will exist in a potentially infinite number of absolutely singular and, consequently, totally unrelated pleasures which, finally, will leave him dispersed. The lover who hopes to deliver himself to his beloved through his surrender to the intensity of her effect on him, then, will find not the object of his desire but the multiplication of desires. He will come to image not the woman he loves but rather the nature of the feminine element itself. He will be inconsistent, dissipated, and trivial.

In Cleland the feminization of the man succeeds not when it simply moves him from one pole of a duality to the other but when it produces a truly androgynous sensibility which comprehends this opposition. In this reciprocity pleasure informs language, frees it from its bondage to conventional meaning, and allows it to speak completely within the particular situation. Language, in turn, extends pleasure and allows it to orient itself in terms of one meaning. Initially this appears as a reconciliation of vision and the bliss of sexuality. When Fanny discovers Charles soon after his return to England, her desire is once more given an object, an image. She faints from the shock of their meeting, and when she recovers she says, "the first object . . . that my eyes open'd on, was their supreme idol, and my supreme wish, Charles" (p. 203). "Absorbed and concentr'ed" (p. 204) in the sight of one another, they exchange "hearts at our eyes" (p. 204). Love, here, is the "refiner of lust" (p. 43) because it focuses pleasure on the object in a way that contains the dispersing movement of pleasure alone. Thus, while love affords the most intimate sensation, "that delicate and voluptuous emotion which Charles alone had the secret to excite" (p. 208), it is one which clearly never turns its back on its cause. In her encounter with Mr. H., "any other man would have been just the same to me" (p. 75). Here, even when she surrenders "every faculty to the sensiblist joys," they affect her "infinitely more with my distinction of the person than the sex" and bring "my conscious heart into play" (p. 208).

Love bridges the loss of pleasure and the fixity of vision; even in the most intense sensation Fanny remains aware of Charles. But it is a different awareness from the one which characterized their first encounter, when Fanny lost her virginity to him. Here Fanny's pleasure is never presented simply as a celebration of his power, and there are none of the sadistic overtones of their first meeting in their reunion. It is not completely absorbed and defined in the object but retains its disruptive, free character. The intensity of their experience leaves Charles and Fanny "voluptuously intermixing" (p. 210). Theirs is a "delightful harmony and concert" (p. 211) which culminates in a moment when "I was he, and he, me" (p. 211). Both submit to the feminine moment of dissolution. They lose themselves in the intensity of this moment. But because, in some way, their hearts remain conscious of the other, their dissolution is contained by the referent. Thus, they lose themselves only to recover themselves in their awareness of the other. The harmony of their sexuality here is the harmonious interplay of masculine and feminine moments.

As stereotyped as these descriptions are, they make clear that Cleland wants something very understandable and familiar. He wants to believe that a man's acceptance of his feminine aspect can, in turn, be extended so that it allows him to understand and speak more directly to the woman he loves. This extension is really the meaning of love for Cleland. In the closing pages of the novel the focus shifts from Fanny, as the locus of a certain sexual experience which becomes the reader's own, to Charles's relation to her and the way we see how a man's acceptance of this experience can mediate between himself and a specific woman. In these pages the relationship of the two takes place on a "higher" level which both contains and transcends the opposition between masculine and feminine. Charles submits to the fragmentation of pleasure and strong emotions only to return to speak a language which is in touch with these. Fanny, in turn, can be reunited with Charles only after her interlude with the elderly gentleman who keeps her after she leaves Mrs. Cole. "Himself a rational pleasurist" (p. 200), he shows her that "the pleasures of the mind were superior to those of the body, at the same time, that they were far from obnoxious to, or incompatible with each other, that . . . the one served to exalt and perfect the taste of the other" (p. 200). On the one hand, this particular formulation obviously privileges the masculine by presenting the reconciliation of language and pleasure as the appropriation of the feminine by the masculine. But if we read this passage in the context of the interchange between Fanny and Charles, in which they exchange masculine and feminine situations, we can see that there is another, more androgynous, dimension to this relationship. This is one in which the continual interplay between masculine and feminine moments allows each to inform the other. What emerges from this interchange is a third consciousness which characterizes both the man who can feel as well as argue and the woman who can speak herself.

This androgynous sensibility allows the argument between the man and the woman to move from confrontation to understanding. He does not try to master the woman; he consults the full range of his experiences as a key to knowing her on her own terms. The perfect coincidence between his desire and its object is effected by this exchange, which does not suppress difference but escapes it while leaving its terms apparently untouched. The couple still experience the difference between masculine and feminine. But they are no longer separated by it because both comprehend this opposition. They have assimilated it, made it their own. When they are reunited, Fanny and Charles are now able to establish a true equality within their marriage. Fanny discovers herself at last bound to Charles in "a subjection of soul, incomparably dearer to me than the liberty of heart which I had been long, too long! the mistress of" (p. 207). But this conventional binding of wife to husband is transformed by the "delightful harmony and concert" (p. 211) which is effected by their "voluptuosly intermixing" (p. 210), which frees them from the stereotyped hierarchical relationship of husband and wife. They can switch roles. When Charles returns he is destitute, "broken down to his naked personal merit" (p. 206). It is Fanny who recognizes and saves him. Charles, in turn, is not judgmental about her life. He can understand her options and would have done the same thing himself. Their marriage is characterized by a cooperative spirit: she makes him rich; he gives her a respectable name. They are man and wife, but they hope to examine marriage in the innocence and equality of perfect understanding.

From this point of view, the ending of *Fanny Hill* becomes a statement of the ability of "communication" to allow us to escape the differences which separate us. By remaining receptive to one another's experiences, Fanny and Charles converse as equals, and this understanding, in turn, makes them well matched. They satisfy one another completely. At the center of this resolution, then, is a certain myth about the power of the private language which develops between the man and the woman as a result of their initial argument. This language is privileged on two counts: first, by its ability to effect satisfaction, to unite lover and woman, personal desire and its specific object, in a moment of mutual comprehension as intense as orgasm yet as stable as marriage; and, second, by the ability of the couple who speaks this language not only to escape the conventional differences of the world but to return to this world and command it. Fanny and Charles, after all, do not retire to a secluded corner to live. They have wealth and position They are not free of the worlds, they are in control of it.

The next two chapters, on *Pamela* and *Les Liaisons dangereuses*, are concerned with two visions of this private conversation. In the first the couple adopt a language of feeling which, like the style of Pamela's journal, reveals the heart. In speaking this language the lover accepts his emotions with the enthusiasm of a recent convert to a formerly despised religion; he finds himself united to his partner in the continuous sympathy which is love. The second version is a negative image of the first. Here, too, the man adopts the woman's attitude, but in this case it is not a feminine one in the sense I have been using this term. In *Les Liaisons dangereuse* Valmont adopts the particularly ironic and detached perspective which Mme. de Merteuol's position gives her on the whole masculine enterprise of seduction. In his dealings with Mme. de Merteuil, Valmont accepts her ironic view of his own masculine project. They become two friends who are too wise to play games with one another, and their wisdom allows them to talk to each other with a clarity of understanding which is free of traditional misconceptions.

Both of these conversational styles, as different as they are, mark that familiar moment when a man believes he is getting to know the woman he desires, so that—either in the expression of feelings or in the exchange of witticisms, which is the conversation of those who are too wise to fall prey to their feelings—he is developing a personal understanding which escapes their stereotyped opposition as man and woman. Both styles are characterized by the way they give the lovers a sense of somehow being above and more powerful than the ordinary world—either more real, more natural (because of the intensity of their emotion) or more clever (because of the clarity of their vision). *Pamela* and *Les Liaisons dangereuses* are each concerned with the establishment of these forms of private understanding, forms which both novels dramatize as the issue of personal correspondence: the exchange in which Pamela gives B her journal; the letters which pass between Valmont and both Mme. de Merteuil and Mme. de Tourvel. But Richardson and Laclos are even more interested in the moment when the man and the woman must turn to the world as a couple and actually experience their understanding. This is the moment, in effect, when this personal exchange comes into conflict with the general circulation of language in the world and must defend itself against this usage.

# III

# Pamela *and the Equality*
# *of Correspondents*

For the reader of *Fanny Hill* the erotic interrupts the thematic in the same way that the woman's gesture in Donne's "The Flea" interrupts the poet's discourse. At its most intense, of course, this interruption is enacted by the gesture of the reader, a gesture which fragments the imagined unity of the reader's sense of physical coherence and reveals it as process, as loss, as feminine. This gesture, too, is not described directly but rather implied in the text. Like the woman's gesture in Donne's poem, it is marginal. It takes place in the space between chapters.

The desire to read pornography in order to be seduced by it is a desire to be interrupted in this way. From this point of view it is easy to see the close relationship between *Fanny Hill* and the appeal of important elements in eighteenth-century literature. In an article on sentimentalism which owes much to his earlier essay on Cleland, Leo Braudy argues that the essential characteristic of the eighteenth-century novel does not lie in some criteria of formal realism which ties it to traditional literary forms and values, but rather in the novelist's attempt to evoke in the reader aspects of "raw and real" experience which lie outside those forms.[1] Hence, the emphasis in the sentimental novel on intense feeling and its desire to "explore those aspects of human nature that resist all the forms that literary tradition can furnish" is, for Braudy, something it shares with earlier novels—including *Fanny Hill*. In a similar context, Malcolm Bradbury writes about Cleland's attempt to evoke the "sexual sublime."[2] In its attention to the reader's experience of disruption, pornography shares the same realm with a literature of the sublime which emphasizes an experience of nature "beyond the capacity of our senses and our understanding to organize and structure it."[3] Both subjectivize the experience of the work, move it from an appreciation of an ordered and formal beauty to the reader's experience of an intense and disruptive moment. In a recent article Richard Kuhns has argued that the eighteenth- and nineteenth-century novel can be read as versions of this argument between the beautiful and the sublime.[4]

Moving from *Fanny Hill* to *Pamela,* we can see how clearly Richardson is a part of this argument. The onset of love in his novels is a moment as shattering in its effects as orgasm. And despite the way this moment brings into question the subject's place in the ordered image of society, Richardson never trivializes it in order to suppress or dismiss. He accepts the reality of passion in the same way that Cleland accepts the reality of sexual desire.

If Richardson shares with Cleland this openness to disruption, he is driven even more intensely by the need to recuperate its loss and find in it some positive meaning. The reasons for this are clear. Think, for a moment, of the different ways in which Fanny and Mr. B. experience desire. Fanny can experience the loss of sexuality for itself because this moment, at its most intense point, turns from the object and frees her from the world. As we have seen, this capacity of pleasure to disengage is somehow behind Fanny and Charles's independence at the end of the novel. But Mr. B experiences love as the loss of emotional stability and control. And while this loss mimics sexuality in the way it disturbs masculine qualities of self-possession, which B's position demands, there is no moment when this intensity turns away from the object. B never surrenders to his feeling as feeling, experiences its intensity the way Fanny gives herself to the intensity of pleasure, without regard to the object which provoked it.

B finds himself feminized by love, but this is a feminine element which can never be experienced, even briefly, as a free and undetermined moment of pleasure. Consequently, it is always subject to the view of the other. And this is particularly true in B's case, because Pamela remains a relentless defender of conventional standards of morality and propriety. She returns B to himself only as a negative meaning, *im*propriety, *im*morality. As a result, B finds himself in a curious place. He must seduce as the feminine seduces. He must disrupt Pamela, disturb her identification with conventional structures, make her sympathetic to the need for immediacy and presence, which is love for Richardson. But this seduction never intends that Pamela should join him in this abandon, which, finally, he experiences only as negation. He wants, really, to elicit some response which will allow him to regain his proper place. He wants to find a form of conversation which will reconcile emotion and language, the lover and the man.

The problem of the lover, from this point of view, is the problem of finding the proper mode of address. The lover is like the writer of familiar letters who wants to establish an intimate correspondence with someone despite an inevitable social or physical distance.

> Who would not choose, when necessary absence . . . deprive her of the person of her charming friend, to have a delight in retiring to her closet, and there, by pen and ink, continue, and, as I may say, perpetuate, the ever agreeable and innocent pleasures that flow from social love, from hearts united by the same laudable ties?
>
> . . . . . . . . . . . . . . . . . . . . . . . . . . . . . . . . . . . . . . . . . . . . . . . . . . . . . . . . . . . . . .
>
> Who then shall decline the converse of the pen? The pen that makes distance, presence; and brings back to sweet remembrance all the delights of presence; which makes even presence but body, while absence becomes the soul . . .[5]

For Richardson this writer, too, describes a paradoxical double movement. On the one hand, familiar letters are the result of an act of retirement in which the writer closets himself from the world. Written "either morning or evening, before needful avocations take place, or after they have been answered" (C, III, p. 247), the letter is composed in solitude. "The pen," Richardson writes, "is jealous of company. It expects, as I may say, to engross the writer's whole self; everybody allows the writer to withdraw: it disdains company; and will have the entire attention" (C, III, p. 247).

Like the lover, the writer is alienated by his desire. He withdraws from the world of the "necessary" and the "needful," which has imposed distance between himself and the other. But, again, it is not a withdrawal to a place which is independent of the social. Richardson's letters lack the meditative quality of a mind reflecting in solitude. Writing never becomes a pleasure which turns away from the world, as this emphasis on withdrawal might suggest. His are always letters in the fullest sense of the word; that is, they are written *to* someone. Even when they are didactic, they are never monologues. On the contrary, they are extremely conversational, filled with comments and questions which invoke the response of the reader.

The writer withdraws, hoping to find an intimacy greater and more intense than that allowed by conventional relations. He does not, however, ask this other to join him in his solitude. He is not interested in creating the conditions of a real presence which would ignore or violate the order of social necessity. If he did he would visit, not write. The intimacy he discovers is one which informs distance while leaving it untouched. It is the intimacy of two people who, while separated, write to one another in a style which "will shew soul and meaning" (C, III, p. 252) in a way that is "indicative, generally beyond the power of disguise, of the mind of the writer" (C, III, p. 244). The pleasures of their correspondence are the "ever agreeable and innocent pleasures that flow from social love, from hearts united" (C, III, pp. 244–45). Theirs is a relationship which supplements rather than shatters propriety. But in the face of its intimacy, actual presence would be "but body" (C, III, p. 246).

The letter is the form in which character manifests itself in Richardson's novels, so it is not surprising that the lover finds himself caught in a tension between distance and presence equivalent to the paradoxical situation of the correspondent. The ambivalence of both situations, finally, is a reflection of Richardson's own feelings about the relationship of the individual and his social context.

> Wise Providence
> Does various parts for various minds dispense:
> The *meanest slaves*, or those who *hedge* and *ditch*,
> Are useful, by their sweat, to feed the *rich*.
> The *rich*, in due return, impart their store;
> Which comfortably feeds the lab'ring *poor*.
> Nor let the *rich* the *lowest slave* disdain:

He's *equally* a *link* of Nature's *chain:*
Labours to the *same end,* joins in *one view;*
And *both alike* the *will divine* pursue.[6]

This passage, which Pamela cites in an attack on Lady Davers's pride, suggests that Richardson saw society as a divinely ordained structure in which all individuals, in fulfilling their "parts," fulfill as well their duty to their fellow humans and to God. What is important, however, is less the presence of this traditional image of society than the particular tonality it takes on in the novel, and as a key to this tonality the poem is somewhat deceptive. The poem suggests that a reciprocity exists between social classes which balances their separation, so that each "Labours to the *same end,* joins in *one view.*" However, there is little of this sense of communion in the novel, little feeling that not only roles but the whole structure of social conventions mediate among people in a positive way.

Instead, Richardson concentrates on the way in which a man's "part" in society allows him to separate himself from others. A word which appears obsessively in *Pamela* is "distance," and one of its important uses is to define the relations among different classes. His jest, Pamela tells B, "is not a jest that becomes the distance between a master and a servant" (p. 29), to which Mrs. Jervis replies, ". . . don't be so pert to his honour: you should know your distance" (p. 29). Pamela answers, "It is very difficult to keep one's distance to the greatest of men, when they won't keep it themselves to their meanest servants" (p. 30). Altogether, the term "distance," or some variation of it, is used in this context sixteen times in the first fifty pages, a frequency which suggests how important this separation is for Richardson and how it overshadows any reciprocity which might exist among classes.

In both *Pamela* and *Clarissa,* however, Richardson uses the term "distance" in another way. According to Pamela, the most important lesson taught to her by Mr. B's mother was to "*keep the men at a distance*" (p. 210). Lady Davers advises Pamela, in a like manner, to "keep the fellows at a distance" (p. 8), and Mr. B asks Mrs. Jervis if Pamela "kept the men at a distance" (p. 11). In these instances "distance" defines the clear area which modesty, or privacy, requires a woman keep between herself and a man.

The separation of the sexes, of masculine from feminine, is mandated by the same system of social conventions which determines the distance among classes. Richardson's emphasis again falls on the power of conventionality to enforce distance and difference rather than on any reciprocity between the sexes. The obsessive sense of privacy and neuralgic sensitivity to the other which characterizes the reaction of Richardson's male and female characters to one another seems, from this point of view, the result of their existence within a system which defines them in such a way that each appears to the other as totally different. They can only see one another as threatening and alien. In this context, codes of modesty and privacy work to protect each individual against the other. This protective function of social forms is particularly clear in *Clarissa*. Here Lovelace's need to "open my whole soul" (p. 375) to Clarissa makes him an enemy not only of the distance between them—"I cannot bear to be kept at this distance from you" (p. 375), he tells her—but also of the social properties which Clarissa, "a *lover of forms*" (p. 245), uses to create this distance.[7] "Had she not thus kept me at arms' length," he writes, "had she not denied me those innocent liberties which our sex, from step to step, aspire to; could I but have gained access to her in her hours of heedlessness and dishabille (for full dress creates dignity, augments consciousness, and compels distance) we had been familiarized to each other long ago" (p. 341). The relation between Clarissa and Lovelace, however, is only a version of that between Pamela and B. It is clear that when B complains to Pamela, during their first meeting in the summerhouse, that "you always fly me when I come near you" (p. 15)—to which she replies, "It does not become your poor servant to stay in your presence, sir, without your business required it; and I hope I shall always know my place" (pp. 15–16)—her implicit assertion of "the distance that fortune made between us" (p. 17) is both the expression of a deeply felt need to enforce a protective separation between them and the statement of a conventional ideology which generates this need by defining B as that which is completely other.

For Richardson, it is precisely because the social structure preserves a certain distance among classes that we are able to remain at ease with one another. But these forms, and the safety they provide, are not sufficient. If they were, there would be no novel entitled *Pamela*. The novel begins with the emergence of another force in the ordered image of society which we find in its pages. It begins, in other words, when the death of B's mother allows all his latent feeling toward Pamela to crystallize and he discovers he loves her.

Love for Richardson is the need to be present to another in an immediate and direct way. It is born of the isolation of a self distanced from others in the same way the writer's movement toward union with his correspondent is born of the solitude of his closet. But the lover, of course, experiences his withdrawal as frustration. Since it does not lead to a union with another, or to the relative liberation of pleasure, his love appears simply as an intolerable sense of frustration at distances which, until now, seemed comfortable and necessary. The birth of love within the ordered distances of society is the great mystery in Richardson's world, and his characters experience it as the presence of an unknown force which, to quote *Pamela*, leaves them "vexed and confused" (p. 17) at their own actions. "But love is not a voluntary thing," Pamela writes. "*Love*, did I say?—But come, I hope not:—At least it is not, I hope, gone so far as to make me *very* uneasy: For I know not *how* it came, nor *when* it began; but crept, crept it has, like a thief, upon me; and before I knew what was the matter, it looked like love" (p. 260).

The tension between the distanced privacy of conventional life and the desire for immediacy, which is love, is central to both Pamela's and B's experience in this novel. But because love comes most violently to B, it is his story which best testifies to its acuteness in Richardson's world.[8]

The fact that we see B through the eyes of Pamela and, consequently, view him primarily as an aggressor obscures the references which suggest that a certain defensive privacy has played an important part in his life. Until he met Pamela, Mr. B was a man who was "averse to matrimony on any terms" (p. 437). His initial objections to marrying Pamela have less to do with his class consciousness than they do with his general reluctance to accept marriage and the involvement it implies. He cannot "endure," he tells Pamela, "the thought of marriage, even with a person of equal or superior degree to myself" (p. 223).

Mr. B's self-sufficient privacy ends during his meeting with Pamela in the summerhouse early in the novel: "I do own to you," he is to tell Pamela later, "that I love you with a purer flame than ever I knew in my whole life; a flame to which I was a stranger; and which commenced for you in the garden" (p. 279). The most immediate effect of this new force in B's life is the destruction of that control which was a result of his distanced situation as Pamela's master. The scene begins with B presenting himself in this role as her master, whose "business does require" (p. 16) her presence. B establishes this position, however, only to be forced by the "purer flame" (p. 279) of love to abandon it. When he seizes Pamela and violates both the actual and the figurative distance between them, he is not acting with the cynical callousness of a rake. His actions are the result of his loss of control in her presence. At this moment, Pamela writes, B looked "I don't know how; wildly, I thought" (p. 16), adding that "he seemed vexed and confused at what he had done" (p. 17).

Later B will explain to Mrs. Jervis that he was "bewitched" by Pamela "to be freer than became me" (p. 29). But this is always the effect Pamela has on B. Even when he seems most in control of the situation, his determination is never equal to the disturbing effect Pamela has on him. Disguised as Nan, the serving girl, he accompanies Pamela to bed, intending to take her by force. But even here, when he seems to have resolved to define conditions on his own terms, Pamela notes that he "trembled like an aspen leaf" (p. 212). B does not see Pamela as a valuable and attractive object which he coolly schemes to possess but as someone who engenders in him a sudden flood of emotion which robs him of all control and mastery.

This movement from reserved master to desiring lover characterizes many of the scenes between Pamela and B. And it is inevitably followed by B's attempt to regain control, either by reasserting his position as Pamela's master or by playing the rake who is merely seducing one of his servants. Both attitudes, however, have the single intention of trivializing Pamela, returning her to the subordinate position of servant and restoring a comfortable distance which will protect B from her effect on him.

From one point of view, these encounters can be described in terms of an intersubjective struggle between the two, in which

B's love forces him to reveal himself to Pamela while she remains concealed. Richardson's own correspondence with one of his many female admirers, Lady Bradshaigh, provides a certain commentary on this aspect of B's situation. Under the assumed name of Belfour, Lady Bradshaigh had written him to plead for a happy ending to *Clarissa*. During the exchange of letters which followed, she was able to maintain this peudonym for over a year, and although their relationship was casual, Richardson was unable to live comfortably with the sense that he was known by Lady Bradshaigh in a way that he did not know her. His letters are filled with intense and repetitious complaints that her refusal to reveal her true identity is founded in a "wantoness of power" (C, IV, pp. 318, 343), that she is a "lover of power" (C, IV, p. 339), and that she is making him "one of her diversions" (C, IV, p. 321).

This exchange of letters reminds us how much Pamela is a book about B and his experience of falling in love with someone who does not immediately reciprocate. But it also makes clear the way in which B's situation is radically different from Richardson's. Lady Bradshaigh and Richardson, after all, are not separated by any great distance in social class, and their sense of addressing one another directly is a function of this. We see "Belfour's" refusal to reveal herself as an expression of personal power because this refusal does not correspond to or assert any conventional difference between them. Its meaning, then, can only be whimsical and subjective.

B and Pamela, of course, are in precisely the opposite position. They face each other across the distance separating master and servant, and we can see that their conversation with one another is, in fact, controlled by the meaning of this difference. We know, for example, that Pamela is not manipulative in the same way that Belfour is. Pamela's silence is meant to express her innocence of any desire for power, any desire to seduce or rise above her station. But B does not read the innocent intention in Pamela's message because her refusal engages all the power of convention to condemn him for violating the proper relationship between master and servant. He never sees her rejection as a passive innocence which could be masking her real regard for him. Instead, it seems aggressive because as a result of it he feels the power of society to condemn. One of the reasons B gives for wanting to send Pamela back to her parents early in the novel is that "it won't be for [my] reputation" (p. 42) to keep her, and throughout much of the book his reaction to her is controlled by her ability to expose him to the judgment of society. Consequently, she seems aggressive and rebellious.

The power of conventional meaning to suppress the personal and intentional is even clearer in Pamela's inability to understand what is most obvious in B's address to her: the fact of a love which is beyond his control and beyond the effects of social distinctions. Consider, for example, the scene that occurs early in the novel when, on the eve of Pamela's planned departure to see her parents, B calls her to him and attempts to "expostulate" (p. 81) with her.

> *He took me up, in a kinder manner than ever I had known;* and he said, Shut the door, Pamela, and come to me in my closet: *I want to have a little serious talk with you.*
>
> . . . . . . . . . . . . . . . . . . . . . . . . . . . . . . . . . . . . . . . . . . . . . . . . . . . . . . . . . .
>
> *Place some confidence in me,* said he: Surely you may, when I have spoken thus solemnly. So I crept towards him with trembling feet, and my heart throbbing through my handkerchief. Come in, said he, when I bid you. I did so. Pray, sir, said I, pity and spare me. I will, said he, as I hope to be saved. He sat down upon a rich settee; and took hold of my hand, and said, *Don't doubt me, Pamela. From this moment I will no more consider you as my servant; and I desire you'll not use me with ingratitude for the kindness I am going to express towards you.* This a little emboldened me; and he said, holding both my hands between his, You have too much wit and good sense not to discover, that I, in spite of my heart, and all the pride of it, cannot but love you. Yes, look up to me, my sweet-faced girl! I *must* say I love you; and *have put on a behaviour to you, that was much against my heart, in hopes to frighten you from your reservedness.* You see I own it ingenuously; and don't play your sex upon me for it. (pp. 81–82)

B is obviously sincere in what he says. He speaks like the lover who, for the moment at least, has given himself to his love. "I must say I love you" (p. 82), he tells her. When he asks Pamela to "place some confidence in me" (p. 81), he asks her to accept his intention at face value. He wants to talk openly, as he would to an equal. And this conversational equality defines the relationship he offers her. "From this moment I will no more consider you as my servant" (p. 81), he says.

B assumes that his love gives him the power to redefine the relationship between them on terms of their own choosing, outside of any public context. The lover's belief in the possibility of this private conversation, in turn, depends on his faith in his ability to state his intentions clearly. The lover believes that he can state his love so that it will be understood as unambiguously as he feels it. Once the woman accepts this message and has confidence in him, their conversation will follow naturally.

Pamela's reactions make it clear, of course, that this does not happen. Initially, she tells us, "I was unable to speak" (p. 82). Then, when her confusion clears, she can reply only "with a down look" (p. 82). "O good sir," she answers, "spare a poor girl that cannot look up to you" (p. 83). As Richardson makes clear in his somewhat allegorical manner, Pamela does not respond to B's intention or accept him at face value because she cannot look him directly in the eyes. She remains a servant and, as such, she hears in his words only the meaning they would have if spoken by a master to a servant. His kindness and openness, in other words, appear as manipulative techniques because the idea of equality remains as unthinkable to her after B's expostulations as it was before. "He will make my poor father and mother's life comfortable" (p. 84), she thinks after he leaves. But she immediately rejects this "obvious" intention in order to interpret his statements in the context of their social difference. "Oh!, said I to myself, that is a rich thought; but let me not dwell upon it, for fear I should indulge it to my ruin—What can he do for *me*, poor girl as I am!—What can his greatness stoop to" (p. 85). Or take her later remark to B: "What proposals can one in your high station make to one in my low one!" (p. 143)

"Strange, d—— fate!" B mutters, "that when I speak so solemnly, I can't be believed!" (p. 83) B makes his offer freely and generously as a sign of his sincerity. But in the context of their relationship as master and servant, the very power he has to do this, to offer equality, emphasizes the fact of their difference, and it is this emphasis which determines for Pamela the mean-

ing of his offer. "My pride of birth and fortune," he continues,
". . . cannot obtain credit with you, but must add to your suspicions" (p. 83). The way in which Pamela hears some inverted
version of what B intends will be familiar to anyone who, for
example, has tried in vain to buy dinner for an unemployed
friend. However sincere the offer, however much you might
want its meaning to be just your good feeling, almost invariably
you will find that your offer has the effect of emphasizing to this
friend that you are employed while he or she is not. It is a rare
situation or relationship which allows us to speak our intentions
directly across some polarizing opposition, such as that between
the employed and the unemployed.

Having just said this, we realize how much the argument here
between B and Pamela is not the result of some localized misunderstanding which could be cleared up in a subsequent conversation. The difference which separates Pamela and B is like all
the conventional differences—masculine/feminine, parent/child,
teacher/student—which separate us from precisely those others to
whom we desire to speak most directly and honestly. In these
situations, again, we all know how easy it is to decide, as B does,
to remove our symbolic masks and say what we really feel. In the
privacy of our own selves we compose long soliloquies in which
we express our true feelings with absolute clarity. But when we
actually speak these unambiguous words to another across some
difference, we find that this other person hears in them, sometimes even more loudly, the voice of the parent speaking to the
child, the man to the woman, or the teacher to the student.

The situation between B and Pamela is not primarily psychological, the result of B's impatience and Pamela's reticence. It is
not, in other words, the result of a conflict of personal qualities.
It is a function of the conventional structuring of their relationship, which marks B's sincerity with the sign of the master so
that Pamela can read in it only the fact of his power, and marks
Pamela's reserve with the sign of social propriety so that B sees
in it only the reflection and condemnation of his own lack of
control. Their frustration is a result of a failure to possess language, to free their expression from a system which determines
not how they express their words and actions but how they are
understood. As long as they attempt to converse within the terms

of this system, this conversation will never be personal in the sense it would be an exchange of purely intentional meanings, an equality of expression and understanding. It will always find itself becoming a conversation between a master and a servant.

Despite his most sincere efforts, then, B lives at the center of a war between love and distance. "He took me in his arms," Pamela writes, "and presently pushed me from him. 'Mrs. Jervis,' said he, 'take the little witch from me; I can neither bear nor forbear her—(Strange words these!)—But stay; you shan't go!—Yet begone!—No, come back again' " (pp. 53–54).

Faced with this dichotomy, B can only try to resolve it by choosing one term and excluding the other. He can, for example, attempt to turn his back on love, allow Pamela to return home, and maintain his former distance from those around him. This alternative describes not only those times when B is actually at the point of allowing Pamela to leave but also those moments when he tries to reassert his position, to become once again simply her master. But this is never really an alternative for him. Although Richardson's characters first experience love as something alien to their lives, it is obviously the manifestation of a need so fundamental that, once awakened, it cannot be denied.

B can, on the other hand, choose the violence of love in all its absolute purity. B has experienced this violence. It has robbed him of control, forced him from his position. But Pamela, of course, retains hers. She remains intact. The most physical of B's advances are intended to redress this imbalance by acts of violence equivalent in their effects on Pamela to the action of love on B himself. B appears as Pamela is preparing for bed. Denied the protective distancing of dress, Pamela will be less able to invoke the difference between them. Kidnapped to Lincolnshire, Pamela will find herself in an ambivalent and undefined place outside society. Faced with the threat of rape, she, too, will tremble like a leaf.

In B's own words to Pamela, these are attempts to "frighten you from your reservedness" (p. 82), to drive her beyond the protective distances of roles to a place where she must confront B directly, react to him as personally as he does to her. But the most aggressive of these attempts, the incident of Pamela's near rape in Lincolnshire, illustrates everything that is ambivalent in Richardson's attitude toward this experience of intensity, which seems outside difference and structure. At this moment Pamela is completely helpless. B kisses her with "frightful vehemence" (p. 212) and his voice breaks upon her "like a clap of thunder" (p. 212). In reaction, Pamela tells us later, she "fainted away quite, and did not come to myself soon, so that they both, from the cold sweats I was in, thought me dying" (p. 213).

On the one hand, B is gratified by the strength of this reaction. It reveals a capacity for passion and feeling which corresponds to his own experience of love. He does provoke in her the same loss of control and mastery which characterizes her effect on him. "I thought I never saw a fit so strong and so violent in my life," he tells Pamela the next day, adding that "what I saw you in once before was nothing to it." But, he continues, "this might be my folly, and my unacquaintedness with what passion your sex *can* shew when they are in earnest" (p. 215). After this moment B is never as paranoid in the face of Pamela's reserve because he no longer sees it as the expression of a fundamental and unambiguous commitment to the limitations of her social position or the manipulative coldness of someone who is trying to use his feelings against him.

Although B is gratified by the intensity of Pamela's reaction, he clearly turns away from this moment. It is enough for him to know that the possibility of this experience is there and that the distance between his confusion and her control of her feelings is not fixed and inflexible. But the actual experience of loss has no real appeal for him. When she is completely defenseless, he does not take her. To B the violence and disruption of sexuality never seems to open onto a space outside difference in the way that Fanny and Charles experience it: as a transcendence of the masculine which can then be recuperated as the grounds for a more harmonious and natural relationship within the social. In fact, the sight of her apparent death robs him of any desire. "My passion for you," he tells her, "was all swallowed up in the concern I had for your recovery" (p. 215).

B's refusal of this moment appears as a concern for Pamela which authenticates the sincerity of his love for her. But this is just the point. B retreats from what is extreme and without limit in this experience. His love seeks an object, someone who will recognize him and answer his demands. But the death of sexuality for Richardson is too violent to be recoverable. The equality B would find with Pamela in the feminine moment of dissolution would be the equality of absolute negation, which could never be extended, lived, or spoken.

The attempt to kidnap and violate Pamela, then, only returns B to a version of his initial situation. In Bedfordshire he had been separated from Pamela by the distance between master and servant, which effectively prevented him from expressing his intentions. When he attempts to move beyond this difference and force a direct intimacy with Pamela, he loses her even more completely to an experience which he can only see as unrecoverable loss. If these were the only alternatives open to B, then he would be forced to endure the inevitable frustration resulting from these distances. But this is not the case. There is another course open to B, a way to finally resolve this conflict. This returns us once more to the nature of personal correspondence.

Remember that for Richardson the situation of the correspondent is a version of the situation of the lover. He withdraws from the "needful associations" (C, III, p. 247) of social life, driven by a desire for a union with another that is more intimate than this world will allow. But the correspondent escapes the frustration of the lover because he discovers a language, a style, which allows this intimacy to coexist within difference. For the correspondent the language of the familiar letter is the instrument which resolves the tension between distance and presence. Because it shows "soul" (C, III, p. 252) it makes each present to the other in a direct way. The couple who write to one another achieve the equality of complete understanding which is illustrated by Richardson's phrase "hearts united" (C, III, p. 244). At the same time, correspondence preserves the difference between them. Protected by this "absence" which "becomes the soul" (C, III, p. 246), they avoid the destructive moment in which identity is lost in the attempt at absolute union.

This ability of familiar style to make "distance, presence" (C, III, p. 246) allows us to understand the role Pamela's journal plays in her marriage to B. Composed largely in the "refuge" (p. 367) of her closet, Pamela's journal is associated with the withdrawal of the writer. It records all her "private thoughts" (p. 236), and, like the familiar letter, records them in a transpar-

ent style. "I don't remember what I wrote," Pamela remarks to
Mrs. Jewkes after B finds her papers, "but I wrote my heart"
(p. 240). Pamela's journal, moreover, not only embodies her
heart but, like a letter, is intended to reveal her heart to another.
It is never the record of a mind meditating on itself and discover-
ing there the principle of its own existence. Even when she is
most isolated, immediately after her kidnapping, she begins her
account, "O My Dearest Father and Mother!" although, she continues, "I have no hope how what I write can be conveyed to
your hands!" (p. 98) When B confronts her with her papers, his
first question is, "To whom . . . are they written?" and she replies, "To my father, sir" (p. 238).

The meaning of Pamela's journal, the message she conveys
when she writes her heart, is, of course, her feelings for B. It
contains her "private thoughts," but these are, finally, "private
thoughts of him" (p. 236). It is inevitable that her journal end in
his hands since, in a real sense, it is written to him. Finally, it is
because the journal makes the distance between them presence
that we can see it does, in fact, act as a letter. The problem between B and Pamela has always centered on the way a face-to-
face encounter hinders conversation. Confronted with one another, both find the intention of their language displaced because
it is read by the other in the context of a social difference which
their actual presence invokes. So B's sincerity is read by Pamela
as a cynical manipulation and Pamela's reticence is read by B as
rejection or disobedience. But since Pamela's writings do embody her "heart" (p. 240), in the absolutely transparent style of
correspondence, they allow her to speak across this difference
and enable B to understand the real meaning of her silence. In
them he finds nothing which is not "innocent, lovely, and uni-
formly beautiful" (p. 317), no "secret of her soul" (p. 227) or
"hidden regard for Mr. Williams" (p. 227) which would give
substance to his paranoia.

This insight releases B's thoughts to turn once again to marriage. But he is free to accept her intention so easily because he
reads in privacy. Although they do talk about her journal together, B never reads it in her actual presence. Even in the scene
where they are discussing Pamela's account of her attempted escape, she insists on withdrawing. "Let me walk about at a little

distance," she tells him, "for I cannot bear the thought" (p. 251). Pamela acknowledges the double function of her journal in the first stanza of the song she sings for Sir Simon.

> "Go, happy paper, gently steal,
> And underneath her pillow lie;
> There, in soft dreams my love reveal,
> That love which I must still conceal
> And, wrapt in awful silence, die."
>
> (p. 313)

Like the "happy paper" of this song, her letters do reveal as they conceal, allowing her to withdraw to a safe remove at the moment of their greatest intimacy. But the same can be said about the way B finally addresses Pamela. The resolution between them is a result of his letter to her. Motivated by the "affection which they [Pamela's papers] have riveted on me" (p. 259), this letter is in every way a response to her journal and an acceptance by B of the role of the correspondent. It is written at a moment when Pamela, returning home, is furthest from him. Yet it is just this distance which implicitly allows her to accept his sincerity and read in his style "so much openness, so much affection, so much honor, too, (which was all I had before doubted, and kept me on the reserve)" (p. 260).

The removal of this last reserve leads Pamela to her first open confession of her love for B. After this point their relationship is never in doubt, and the meaning of this seems clear. In Richardson's world B and Pamela must first become correspondents before they can marry. But the real effect of familiar style appears not so much in the way it resolves the distance between master and servant as in the way it allows Pamela and B to live the no less distanced and formal relation of husband and wife. As B explains to Pamela, he has always wanted a relationship with a woman which escaped the confines of conventional possibilities. "I believe I am more nice than many gentlemen [in his choice of a wife]," he tells her, "but it is because I have been a close observer of the behaviour of wedded folks, and hardly ever seen it to be such as I should like in my own case" (p. 472). Specifically, B objects to those marriages which accept the inevitability of opposition between husband and wife. "Had I married with the views of many gentlemen," he continues, ". . . I had wedded a fine lady, brought up pretty much in my own manner, and used to have her will in everything" (p. 472). Such liaisons inevitably become power struggles, which can only end in the ambivalence of compromise. "Some gentlemen can come into a compromise; and, after a few struggles, sit down tolerably contented. "But," he adds, "had I married a princess, I should not have done so" (p. 472). B rejects the way such a compromise preserves the difference between man and woman or husband and wife. This opposition will always act as a limit on their relationship.

For B this is not enough. Before he marries, he tells Pamela, he must love, and his love will not accept this difference, this opposition. To have married, he continues, "I must have been morally sure, that she preferred me to all men; and to convince me of this, she must have lessened, not aggravated my failings" (p. 472). In other words, B will not accept a wife who becomes an opponent searching for his weaknesses. It would be easy, in this light, to read him as a man who wants to have his way without having to work for it. But his reasons for rejecting struggle and compromise make his attitude not necessarily something more than but something different from a simple statement of unrestrained willfulness. B's real objection is not to his frustration at losing in specific situations but to the way a wife's opposition in these situations would establish some more fundamental difference between them. B does not dream of omnipotence. He dreams of an equality between himself and his wife, a reciprocity which would transcend any possible difference. "My wife," he says, "should not have given cause for any part of my conduct to her to wear the least aspect of compulsion or force. The word *command*, on my side, or *obedience* on hers, I would have blotted from my vocabulary" (p. 473). For B the idea of the argument between husband and wife as a kind of intimate conversation across opposition is inconceivable, and he does not want to have to win obedience in the give-and-take of such a struggle. Even if he won repeatedly, the fact of resistance would rob him of any satisfaction. He wants love to act as a unifying element which makes the issues of power and the differences between husband and wife or master and servant irrelevant.

By enabling Pamela and B to address one another directly, apart from the opposition and difference imposed by convention, familiar correspondence allows this agreement of lovers to take place. This exchange opens the way for the reciprocity which Richardson desired with Lady B to exist between them. Communication in this sense implies the fundamental agreement and identity with the other we assume when we say we understand someone else's point of view. As this phrase suggests, understanding here is more fundamental than the fact that we may stand in opposition to one another. Thus, on those "*small points* in dispute, from which the greatest quarrels among friends generally arise," B desires that his wife never differ from him "for *contradiction-sake,* but . . . to convince me for *my own*" (p. 473). Pamela comments on this injunction, saying that "as both will find their account in this, if one does, I believe it is very just" (p. 478). B's concern, then, is less with having his way in all matters, however small, than in suppressing the larger emotional effect of contradiction. It is his duty, he says, to desire nothing of his wife that is not significant, reasonable, or just (p. 473). B accepts limits on his prerogatives but forbids a contradiction whose function is, by opposing, to establish the other as difference. He wants to find a natural agreement with the other within which any difference will be just a brief and trivial moment.

Such an understanding would be possible, of course, only if each was continually assured of the good faith of the other. Since the agency of this mutual understanding is the journal, it is not surprising that B asks Pamela to continue her writing even after their marriage. The last half of Richardson's novel records the formalization of their relationship and its reconciliation with convention. They define their duties toward one another as husband and wife and begin the difficult task of introducing Pamela to society. B abandons the sentimental and feminine role of the lover subject to the woman and reassumes his place in the masculine order. He becomes a "daring and majestic [figure] as courageous as a lion" (p. 481). B's anger is so intense that when he is upset, Pamela must never dare "intrude" (p. 481) upon him. Pamela, in turn, withdraws and diminishes to a respectful and yielding position. Their life is arranged according to the hierarchical differences between husband and wife. They accept a given distance between them which marks, again, a certain opposition in their roles.

But in the context of their exchange of journal and letter, their relationship as husband and wife becomes assimilated to their relationship as correspondents. This difference does not structure their life the same way the distance between master and servant initially did. It does not cast them as opponents. Instead, this opposition is itself mastered by the agreement between those who read and write to one another. It does not define them; they define it. Their correspondence allows them to assimilate the formal relationship of marriage and to make the conventional personal.

The importance of correspondence is not in the way the actual exchange of journal and letter between B and Pamela allows some practical resolution of their situation but in the way this exchange generates a certain kind of conversation for which the situation of correspondents is only a model. In this relationship difference is no longer confronted directly. B no longer wants to have Pamela and the sexual tension between them disappears, really, as soon as they read one another. B's desire for the immediate and physical possession of her has been replaced or satisfied by his understanding of her. Within the equality and unity of their understanding they are allowed to differ with one another and to live at some distance as long as these disagreements are trivial and never become the sign of some ultimate difference which intrudes on their fundamental agreement.

It is clear from the way their marriage allows Pamela and B to establish an equality within difference that they are enacting the historical movement in the eighteenth century toward ideals of "companionate marriage"[9] and "heterosexual friendship"[10] documented by Lawrence Stone and Jean Hagstrum. Both scholars emphasize how Richardson's contemporaries increasingly hoped to find, within the traditional distinction between husband and wife, a reciprocal conversation with an other who has become friend and equal. Stone, for example, quotes the popular *A Letter of Genteel and Moral Advice to a Young Lady* (1740) by Wetenhall Wilkes as a typical statement of this ideal: "This state with the affection suitable to it, is the completest image of heaven we can receive in this life; the greatest pleasures we can enjoy on earth are the freedoms of conversation with a bosom friend . . . When the two have chosen each other, out of all the species, with a design to be each other's mutual comfort and entertainment . . . all the satisfactions of the one must be doubled because the other partakes in them."[11]

In Stone's analysis the companionate marriage is itself the product of the emergence in the seventeenth century of what he terms "affective individualism," which encourages men to maximize their pleasure and satisfaction in political, social, and economic spheres. This emphasis on the freedom of the desiring individual modifies, in turn, the patriarchical model of marriage and opens it up to a wider range of emotional and sexual relations between husband and wife, relations which are not absolutely consistent with their hierarchical opposition. In a similar manner, Hagstrum's idea of heterosexual friendship concentrates on the way the acceptance of affectionate conversation and sexual desire between husband and wife alters traditional models, which devalued erotic relationships between the sexes and made them the sign of an essentially effeminate lust on the part of the man. His reading of Milton's divorce tracts emphasizes how Milton turned away from a tradition of Christian astheticism which, since Augustine, had suppressed the husband's erotic relationship to his wife as a denigration of his intellectual and spiritual nature.[12]

Hagstrum's commentary reminds us of how the equality of man and woman in marriage implies the equality of masculine and feminine within the individual. The woman is no longer silent and obedient but must speak her feelings. The man is no longer cold, withdrawn, and controlled but must give himself to his desires and emotions. To experience marriage as an intimate friendship each must accept the other within himself or herself as a precondition to accepting the other in marriage. B's reconciliation with Pamela is made possible, finally, because their correspondence allows him to reconcile himself to his own feminine nature. As we have seen, from the very opening pages of the novel his hostility toward Pamela is a function of the way in which the effect of her presence emasculates him, forces him to act on needs and desires inconsistent with the coherence and control his position as master demands. He experiences the war between distance and presence most intimately as the opposition between a masculine reserve, within which he can no longer live comfortably, and a feminine experience of intense and disruptive emotion, which threatens to end, finally, in a moment of loss and annihilation in which the masculine is eradicated. By allowing his desire to be displaced into language, the style of Pamela's journal allows B to reconcile this opposition. He can now reveal himself within the context of conventional relationships; he is free to express his needs openly, while at the same time remaining "as courageous as a lion" (p. 481). His love for Pamela no longer divides him in such a manner that his feelings are opposed to his manhood. Rather, they are its natural complement, its other but equal side.

In this way *Pamela* makes clear how the imaginary of marriage as a blissful state is dependent on an understanding and a manner of conversing which exists both within and beyond difference. Pamela's genius is to be able to write in such a style, which expresses feeling in a manner that allows B to accept that other which he finds within himself and, consequently, frees him to accept Pamela herself. On the one hand, the language of familiar correspondence is completely "natural." It is an instinctive language of the heart which is beyond conscious intention. Not only is it beyond the power of the writer to disguise, it is beyond the power of rational argument to resist. When B reads her journal, he is not persuaded but touched, moved to respond as unreflexively as her language and as intimately as the effect on him of her physical presence. The rhythms of expression and understanding mimic the interplay of touch and response in sexuality. Love seems to find its natural end in sympathy just as sexual desire does in orgasm.

But, on the other hand, even the most intense feeling which can be written can be understood and controlled. Pamela has always had access to this style, and it has always given her this control. Love made B hysterical, but it only made Pamela write, and because she could write she retained her self-possession. When B reads her journal and adopts her style, when he writes his heart in the letter which returns her to him, he also accepts his feelings. He becomes calm and they arrange their life together in terms of their mutual understanding.

In B's acceptance of this familiar style we can see something of Richardson's own choice of the form and subject of his novel. Both Richardson and B seem to offer themselves here as examples of men who no longer define themselves in opposition to women. Instead of a language of mastery, they speak a language which recognizes the feminine, which accepts and accommodates itself to the flow of emotion. They agree to understand women on their own terms, to be willing partners in a relationship which, like the reciprocity between lovers in "The Good-morrow," establishes an essential androgynous equality between partners in the midst of conventional difference. But if both B's acceptance of Pamela's journal and the novel *Pamela* itself can be read as a willingness on the part of men to accept and understand their other, it is curious to see how both offers are implicitly compromised in the course of the last half of the novel. B is not content with the way the journal allows him and Pamela to resolve their differences, and it does not exist for long simply as the model for a certain kind of personal conversation which allows them to redefine the traditional relation between husband and wife within the privacy of their own marriage. If this were all that was involved, they would remain at B's country estate in Lincolnshire. But B plans a life in London and Bath. He intends that they live and circulate in society, and this implies not only that they will read each other but that they will be read by this larger world in which they intend to take their place. To this world Pamela will remain a servant who has been clever enough to marry her master, and B will be looked upon as a master who has been foolish or arrogant enough to believe he can raise a servant to his own level. They will be able to escape the judgment of society, the judgment which its gossip will pass on them, only if its members come to understand B and Pamela the way they have come to understand one another.

This necessity explains why, suddenly, these most private papers are made public. They precede her into the world, where they become the agency of this larger acceptance. Initially Lady

Davers is forced to acknowledge Pamela because she fears her brother's anger. But her true reconciliation will be an effect of the journal. "It must be a rare and uncommon story," she remarks when she asks Pamela for her papers, "and will not only give me great pleasure in reading, but will entirely reconcile me to the step he has taken" (pp. 483–84). And it is not only Lady Davers who will read Pamela's journal. B's sister will take these writings to London, where, according to Pamela, "she intends to entertain Lady Betty with, and another lady or two, her intimates, as also her Lord; and hopes to find, in the reading of them, some excuse for her brother's choice" (p. 486).

At the point it enters wider circulation, Pamela's journal becomes more than the example of a form of intimate communication between two correspondents who know one another personally. The journal's power to speak intimately across difference is generalized and becomes the power of a certain literary style to address readers directly, aside from any ongoing personal relationship they might have with the author. Because it reveals Pamela's heart "beyond the power of disguise" (C, III, p. 244), her writing can validate her, express her feelings with a sincerity which commands understanding and sympathy from those who are not personal acquaintances. Here the style of familiar correspondence loses any supplementary, subservient relationship to conventional language, and the distinctions which the latter maintains, to become instead the mistress of this language. Freed from the immediate context of actual correspondence, Pamela's journal can address others without regard to these distinctions. Since it expresses intentionality in an absolutely transparent way, it can force readers to understand the emotional reality of a situation rather than simply gossip about the way it appears to them.

Because it has an absolute power of expression, the familiar style can define and force conventional judgment to yield to its perception. Pamela's journal will precede her to Lady Betty's, where it will be read and accepted. Pamela and B will later appear to occupy the place it has secured for them. They will be read in the context of their writings, like successful authors on a talk show. B, in fact, has always described Pamela's journal as a story they are composing together. "There is such a pretty air of romance, as you relate them, in your plots and my plots," he tells her after he has read the first part of her journal, "that I shall be better directed in what manner to wind up the catastrophe of the pretty novel" (p. 242). Lady Davers reads these papers in precisely this way. She will, she tells Pamela, "take great pleasure to read all his stratagems . . . on the one hand and all your pretty counterplottings . . . for it must be a rare and uncommon story" (p. 482).

By the close of *Pamela*, the personal style has, effectively, become a form of authorial address in which this author masters and imposes his intention on a passive readership not by the force of argument but by a particularly powerful appeal to their "natural" feelings and sympathy. The ambivalence of this language, in other words, has been employed so that the feminine can be made to express a masculine intention. It is not accidental, from this point of view, that its first outside reader will be Lady Davers, who will be silenced and put in her place by its power to move. Behind this transformation we can see the failure of understanding to maintain itself against the ability of conventional difference to reassimilate any attempt to transcend its oppositions. Understanding requires that B accept and comprehend the other in a way which makes the latter no longer antagonistic but allows it to exist as other. But once he does accept the feminine in himself and in Pamela, once this acceptance is spoken and becomes explicit, so that his feelings for her no longer intrude and disrupt, he experiences the feminine only as something known, fixed, and mastered. In this way understanding becomes simply an expression of a conventional masculine position.

This is true not only because we inevitably hear this intention in B's voice and actions toward the end of the novel. It is also true because the sense of explicit understanding has a seductive effect on B himself, leads him to see himself as even more majestic and powerful because he is now in touch with his feelings. So, when he turns to express his understanding to the world, he feels it as a kind of declaration of independence which authorizes him to command that this world take the shape of his desire. In this transformation the feminine succumbs to a masculine which, rather than confronting it directly, pretends to talk its language, to allow it to have its own space, only to discover that this apparent sympathy is only another form of domination. The mas-

culine adopts the feminine as a disguise, an instrument, a style
which can be assumed in order to seduce the other to accept the
formalization of an explicit understanding.[13]

The problem of the man who wants to be sympathetic to
women, the man who shows his own feminine side and, to some
degree, identifies with them, rests, finally, on this question of the
ability of understanding to maintain itself against a conventional
opposition which always defines understanding as possession and
conquest. And this is a problem which, obviously, extends beyond any narrow concern with any single individual's conscious
intention to address the way in which intention and sincerity are
always at the mercy of more powerful symbolic structures. From
this perspective it is hardly surprising that Richardson's attention
shifts from the relatively simplistic and naive figure of B to the
more complex character of Lovelace, the apparently reformed
rake who experiences this problem in a particularly intense way.

In this context it is interesting to juxtapose *Pamela* and Laclos's
*Les Liaisons dangereuses*. Writing some forty years after the publication of *Pamela*, Laclos knew Richardson's novels, and his
work is concerned with many of the same themes: seduction,
of course; the relationship established by correspondence; the desire to control the judgments of gossip by controlling the circulation of manuscripts and letters; and the "natural" sympathy of
lovers. Laclos is particularly intrigued by the movement by means
of which understanding apparently transcends difference, only to
be fascinated by a vision of its own power, so that it destroys the
equality it has worked to define. More than any character in the
novels of Richardson, Valmont, the central male figure in *Les
Liaisons dangereuses*, illustrates the complex inevitability of this
process. Valmont is a man who, for all his masculine prowess, still
desires to live beyond the limits of this position. Consequently he
seems to search for himself in an understanding relationship with
the feminine. In this way he is drawn to surrender himself to an
emotion for Mme. de Tourvel which promises to carry him beyond these limits. But Valmont is also attracted to that other way
the feminine seems to stand outside the masculine, namely, the
way a feminine sense of the arbitrariness of masculine structures
and masculine power manifests itself not only in a relentless anger
but also in a piercing irony whose detachment allows women to

exercise a power in the world no less effective because it cannot be explicit. In his relationship with Mme. de Merteuil Valmont seems to accept and understand her ironic sense of his own masculinity. He is both the ironic and the sentimental lover, and because he is concerned with these dual ways in which a man can sympathize with the feminine *Les Liaisons dangereuses* is a particularly appropriate sequel to *Pamela*.

# IV

## Les Liaisons dangereuses *and* the Myth *of* the Understanding Man

*Les Liaisons dangereuses* IS THE STORY of two seducers and two seductions. In one case the Vicomte de Valmont pursues the absolutely virtuous Mme. de Tourvel. Initially he is motivated by the desire for a conquest which will crown his reputation as a *libertin*. But their relationship soon becomes a love story in which Valmont seeks to escape the ephemerality of momentary triumphs and pleasures in the warmth of feeling. Finally he gives himself to Mme. de Tourvel and accepts her feeling as his own. The story of Valmont and Tourvel, then, concerns the role of sensation and emotion in forming a relationship and establishing the continuous sympathy between partners which we know as love.

In the other case Valmont and his former mistress, the Marquise de Merteuil, conspire to ruin Cécile Volanges, the young fiancée of their common antagonist, the Comte de Gercourt. Valmont and Merteuil have found the wisdom to put love behind them. They have seen that the game played between men and women, which pits the male's power and mastery against the female's ability to provoke pleasure and feeling, is dictated by their conventional relationship rather than by their innate abilities and natures. This awareness, in turn, allows Valmont and Merteuil to accept one another as equals, to become friends instead of opponents, and they converse with the cool and lucid detachment of people who have thoroughly examined their situation and long ago eliminated any grounds for disagreement. They understand one another perfectly, and their understanding gives them unique power. Because they see that the conventions of their world are a game, they can play it with unparalleled success. The mastery which each exercises is all the more effective because each is self-aware and free of any illusions. The story of Valmont and Merteuil, then, is about the belief that our ability to comprehend our world will liberate us from its determining action and deliver it to us as our own.

In juxtaposing these two narratives, *Les Liaisons dangereuses* presents the ambivalence of seduction with special clarity. Here we see again how it can lead either to an experience of mastery or to a surrender to the intensity of feeling, either the masculine or the feminine. As in *Fanny Hill* and *Pamela*, this ambivalence creates an area of sexual ambivalence apparently outside the conventional restriction of these qualities to the male and the female, respectively, a space where men can feel and women can enjoy the prerogatives of power. For Valmont the seduction of Tourvel becomes a way to discover his capacity for a feminine sympathy with another, whereas for Merteuil seduction allows her to speak and act with the defining force of the masculine and to address Valmont as his equal.

The fascination which the whole project of seduction exercises in these novels lies not only in themes of sexuality and possession, which are associated with the direct confrontation of men and women over their difference. It is also in the awareness of seduction as a possible way around this difference and toward an understanding which is free of its negative effects, a conversation which is not an argument or a form of equality which trivializes the opposition of the sexes. *Les Liaisons dangereuses* presents us with two versions of this conversation, the language of sympathy and the language of understanding, which together incorporate our assumption that we can escape difference either by the force of our intelligence or the strength of our feelings. *Fanny Hill* and *Pamela* end with the discovery of some version of these languages as a possible solution. Laclos, however, subjects both alternatives to a particularly cold and analytical examination. The sympathetic understanding of the feminine and the analytic understanding of the masculine are set against one an-

other, made rivals for the attention of Valmont, who, in his relations with Tourvel and Merteuil, must speak to both of them. In
this situation of rivalry, each speaker questions the other's pretensions to exist outside difference because each hears in the other
only the conventional relationship between men and women. The
plot of *Les Liaisons dangereuses* turns on the ability of each narrative to deflate the other's assumptions and to show that even
the most intense sympathy and the most detached analysis find
themselves subject to the most common differences. But to understand this process we must examine in greater detail the nature
of these conversations.

> I say "*my* principles" intentionally. They are not, like those of
> other women, found by chance, accepted unthinkingly, and fol-
> lowed out of habit. They are the fruit of profound reflection. I
> have created them: I might say that I have created myself.
>
> (LXXXI)[1]

Merteuil claims for herself the most radical freedom, the freedom
to define herself as an absolutely unique meaning. She is "the fruit
of profound reflection" and dependent on nothing outside herself.
But when the reader encounters this passage in the context of the
long and famous letter in which Merteuil describes for Valmont
the history of this self-invention, he is struck by a paradox. Her
project has involved the most meticulous study of the two systems of convention which govern her world, the code of morality
and the code of love. In the year following her husband's death
she writes, "I studied our manners in the novelists, our opinions
in the philosophers; I went to the strictest moralists to find out
what they demanded of us, so as to know for certain what it was
possible to do, what it was best to think, and what it was necessary to seem to be." And a few lines later she adds that after a
year of mourning and study, "I felt the need of coquetry to
reconcile me once more to love; not in order to feel it, of course,
but in order to inspire it and pretend to be inspired. In vain had I
been told and had I read that it was impossible to feign the feeling; I have already observed that to do so one had only to com-
bine an actor's talents with a writer's wit" (LXXXI).
Merteuil claims to find the freedom of the novelist who writes
her own story within the discipline of an actor who studies a

script in order to reenact it. While these claims might seem paradoxical, they do not, at least initially, seem contradictory. Merteuil is, without a doubt, the most singular individual in *Les Liaisons dangereuses*. Yet this singularity never takes the form of flagrant unconventionality. No one seems more at home in her world.

In *Beginnings* Edward Said suggests one way to formulate the tension between what is unique and what is determined in Merteuil's position. For Said the European novel is characterized by the opposition of two principles. The first, which he calls "authority," expresses the "appetite" that Western writers "develop for modifying reality."[2] It designates, in this case, Merteuil's assumption of the power, the authority, to create and determine meaning. The antagonistic tendency, which Said terms "molestation" designates the author's awareness of all elements—physical, social, and psychological—which resist and intrude upon the innovative projects of this fantasy.[3]

For Said the power of individual authority to modify reality is intimately related to the ability of irony to free itself from a simple, mimetic repetition. Irony repeats, but always with a difference, "making repetition itself the very form of novelty."[4] From Said's point of view Merteuil's position appears as a certain version of this ironic repetition, one which acknowledges conventionality's demand that its forms be imitated exactly but makes this repetition the medium of a new life, a created self—in Said's terms a beginning.

Merteuil's position, then, is the classic position of the novelist. The year following her husband's death she is like Cervantes languishing in jail with the unpublished manuscript of *Don Quixote*. He, too, has a vision of a radical individuality, but, as he tells us, he is prevented from publishing it because, on the one hand, the laws of literary convention require that a book have learned footnotes and, on the other, the law of nature which ordains that like begets like dictates that his book, the "child" of his uneducated wit, have none.

Cervantes is stymied by the apparently fixed and necessary relationship between nature and convention. The world of language is tied to the mimetic repetition of the natural world. The wisdom of the ancients, which, in the form of dedicatory epistles and footnotes, certifies the validity of a book, derives its authority from the fact that this wisdom is accepted as a reflection of the natural order. In such a system the imaginations of the individual can have only the fantastic and marginal existence of uncirculated manuscripts kept in the bottom drawers of desks.[5]

Cervantes is freed from this impasse—and *Don Quixote* from this fate—by a friend who points out that it is not necessary that Cervantes's book be learned. It is enough that he invent the appropriate editorial machinery so that it appear learned. This moment is not discussed at great length, but it is, in effect, Cervantes's explanation of the novel's existence. It dramatizes the way in which *Don Quixote* implies the detachment of language from the identity of things and the relocation of its function in the power to represent, to orchestrate an illusory resemblance between the "real" and its repetition in language. The conventions which govern publication no longer authenticate the truth of a book. They are "simply" conventions which determine the way a book must present itself in order to circulate. Convention determines a form of representation. But since this form is no longer inevitably fixed to a natural meaning, it appears to be something that can be played with. Cervantes reproduces these conventions the way an actor reproduces a script, that is, with an awareness of its fictional nature. And this awareness allows him to repeat these conventions ironically so that they are freed from their former meaning and become the vehicle for a radically different intention.[6]

Merteuil's blending of the talents of actor and author points to an equally radical redefinition of the conventional meaning of woman. Seduction, for her, *is* this process of redefinition, but in order to understand this we have to understand how her seductions differ in important ways from the many other affairs which take place in the novel. From her point of view it is clear that the libertine world is not an area of free sexuality which escapes the structuring effect of traditional morality. Morality is a system which takes upon itself the authority to define the nature of male and female and determine their interaction. In *Les Liaisons dangereuses* it decrees that a wife will be subject to her husband, but it also determines that a woman will be no less subject to her lover. After all, as Merteuil writes to Valmont, ". . . promises reciprocally given and received can be made and broken at will by you alone: we are lucky if upon an impulse you prefer secrecy to scandal, if, content with a humiliating submission, you stop short of making yesterday's idol the victim of tomorrow's sacrifice" (LXXXI).

At the center of this subjection of woman by man is a conventional definition of the feminine which explains a woman's vulnerability by relating it to a supposed natural susceptibility to sensation and emotion. In her autobiographical letter to Valmont, Merteuil explicitly defines herself against the two most common classes of women, those "who call themselves women of *feeling*" and "those whom you call sensitive; who are always so easily and so powerfully moved to love." The first of these, "with their stupid delusions, imagine that the man with whom they have found pleasure is pleasure's only source; and, like the superstitious, accord that faith and respect to the priest which is due to only the divinity." Women in the second group suppress their susceptibility to pleasure but do so only to give themselves to emotion with an equivalent recklessness. They surrender themselves "completely to the fermentation in their minds [and] give birth as a result to letters full of tenderness but fraught with danger; and who are not afraid to confide these proofs of their weakness to the person responsible for them: imprudent creatures, who cannot see in the lover of today the enemy of tomorrow" (LXXX). In both cases the signs which mark their surrender to pleasure or emotion are read as the expression of woman's innate dependence on man, who, as the source of her pleasure and love, has the authority to define her as he chooses.

Merteuil's seductions are aimed precisely at this apparently natural inequality between the sexes. She sees these positions—male/female, powerful/weak—as relative ones which can be assumed by any two individuals rather than the expression of inherent characteristics. Yet she does not attempt to transform this situation by confronting it directly and stripping away the illusion of the natural. She employs a reversing irony which always remains couched within the rules of this conventional relationship. Behind the screens of moral widow and pliant mistress she works to assume the power attributed to the male. This is the real point she makes in her autobiographical letter to Valmont.

His triumphs, she remarks, are simply extensions of the power over women which society "naturally" attributes to men. She, on the other hand, seeks a more radical victory. She would turn "the formidable male into the plaything of my whims and fancies" (LXXXI).[7]

Merteuil's project begins with her suppression of the supposedly innate sensitivity and sensibility which make women subject to male authority. In an important passage Valmont's aunt, Mme. Rosemonde, formulates this conventional relationship in the following way: "A man enjoys the happiness he feels, a woman the happiness she gives. This difference, so essential and so little noticed, yet influences the whole of their respective conduct in the most remarkable way. The pleasure of one is to satisfy his desires, of the other, it is, above all, to arouse them" (CXXX). Here, again, it is in the nature of things that satisfaction, like power, always passes to the man. It is the mark of his "natural" superiority.

In the letter which follows, however, Merteuil paraphrases Mme. de Rosemonde in an illuminating way. Writing to Valmont, she remarks:

> Have you not yet observed that pleasure, which is undeniably the sole motive force behind the union of the sexes, is nevertheless not enough to form a bond between them? And that, if it is preceded by desire which impels, it is succeeded by disgust which repels? That is a law of nature which love alone can alter: and can love be summoned up at will? Nevertheless, love is necessary, and the necessity would really be very embarrassing had not one perceived that fortunately it will do if love exists on one side only. The difficulty is thus reduced by half without much being lost thereby: in fact one party enjoys the happiness of loving, the other that of pleasing—the latter a little less intense it is true, but to it is added the pleasure of deceiving, which establishes a balance; and so everything is satisfactorily arranged. (CXXXI)

In Merteuil's formulation the conventional relationship is apparently preserved. There is one partner—from Mme. de Rosemode's point of view the man—who receives pleasure and one partner who gives it. But here the meaning of these roles has been reversed. The state of the one who receives pleasure is mystification, the persistence of enjoyment being the result of an illusory extension of the moment of natural pleasure. Merteuil's use of the term "love" here would seem to include, by implication, any form of the belief by men that their pleasure certifies their conventional authority and power over women. The traditional role of the woman, on the other hand, has become the position of power. Although she sacrifices the intensity of physical pleasure, this loss is recuperated in her ability to deceive the mystified male.

This passage explains why Merteuil never gives herself to the moment. Even on her wedding night, she writes, "I took exact account of pains and pleasures, regarding my various sensations simply as facts to be collected and meditated upon" (LXXXI). Merteuil has taken the traditional devaluation of woman's pleasure which Mme. de Rosemonde formulated so well and made it the vehicle for a rigorous suppression of sensation and emotion which has quite another effect. This suppression breaks the "natural" relationship between feelings of pleasure and love, on the one hand, and the expression of these feelings, on the other, which binds women to their traditional role. The forms and signs of expression become merely conventions which, like the footnotes and dedicatory epistles of *Don Quixote*, can be manipulated and made to serve a different meaning. Merteuil is most proud, perhaps, of her ability to free these signs from any possible connection with the natural reality of her experience. "When I felt annoyed," she writes to Valmont, "I practised looking serene, even cheerful; in my enthusiasm I went so far as to suffer pain voluntarily so as to achieve a simultaneous expression of pleasure" (LXXXI). Merteuil surrenders any identification with the immediacy of sensation and feeling, but she exists on a level of privileged conventionality, privileged because she defines *its* meaning rather than it defining *hers*.

In this way Merteuil enacts traditional roles ironically so that the apparently passive and determined female becomes a center of power. This is nowhere more clear than in Merteuil's encounter with Prévan, Valmont's only real rival. The former has wagered with friends that he can seduce Merteuil, who society believes to be as frigid as she is virtuous. In his approach, however, Prévan is made vulnerable by his literal acceptance of the clichés of his world. For all his sophistication, he accepts without question the belief that the vulnerability of women and the power of men are fixed by their natures and he operates within these limits. Like the barber in *Don Quixote*, who believes that the word "basin" expresses the immutable nature of the object, Prévan has absorbed the wisdom of his world but is blind to its assumptions and, consequently, to what might fall outside its limits. He interprets Merteuil's glances and the pressure of her hand as signs that she has been possessed by feelings for him that will eventually overpower her. But to Merteuil, of course, these are part of a completely predictable game which she watches from a distance. "Manner of arrival, behavior, attitude, choice of language," she writes of Prévan, "I knew about them all the evening before" (LXXXV). By appearing to succumb in an equally predictable way, she is able to compromise Prévan while, to all outward appearances, retaining her own innocence.

But Merteuil's control of this situation requires a rigorous denial of any pleasure it might afford. At one point near the end of this little drama, Prévan has hidden himself in Merteuil's bedroom while she remains at the party downstairs. During this evening she considers escaping the boredom of an endless game of cards by joining him briefly. "I was thus on the path to destruction when it occurred to me that, once I had completely surrendered, I should no longer have sufficient power over him to keep him to that appearance of decency so necessary to my plans" (LXXXV). The acceptance of physical pleasure would destroy Merteuil's freedom. She would become her feelings in the same way that other women are only their feelings, and Prévan would have the last word. "She is just like all the rest," he would say.

But Merteuil retains her control and determines the final interpretation of this incident. "It is to my solitude that you owe this long letter," she tells Valmont in closing her narrative. "I shall now write one to Madame de Volanges, who is sure to read it out in company, whereupon you will hear the story again as adapted for publication" (LXXXV). As a result, it is Prévan who is dishonored, ruined, banished.

In this incident Merteuil assumes the role of the man and disposes of Prévan as if he were a woman. We can see clearly how her effectiveness is a result of her systematic analysis of the social structure of her world. Her power is the reward for her years of careful study of the nature and subtleties of convention, and her position rests on the assumption that such study can free us from those forces which act to determine our lives. By subjecting them to a detached analysis we will comprehend them, and in comprehending them we will escape their effect. Instead of being the product of our world we will be our understanding of its system of production.

In Merteuil the distance of irony is coupled with the detachment of the theorist who stands outside a system and discusses it in a language free of its illusions. This is the basis of her correspondence with Valmont. Their relationship is unique because in his dealings with her Valmont, too, adopts an ironic, sophisticated distance from the conventions of his world. Together they have agreed to sacrifice any continuing sexual or emotional relationship. In doing so Valmont suspends the prerogative of the man over the woman, and in suspending them he acknowledges to her that he realizes these prerogatives are artificial rather than a function of a natural difference between male and female. The conversation between Valmont and Merteuil is a conversation between two people who share the same clearly defined theoretical position. Their understanding lifts them above the mystifying struggle of their world, where men must continually affirm their omnipotence by ruining women and women must continually attempt to possess the source of their pleasure and feelings by inspiring men to love them.

Valmont and Merteuil, in other words, no longer have to argue because in their relationship they need not define themselves against one another within the opposition between masculine and feminine. They share, instead, a common understanding of the conventional nature of this difference and correspond in the clear, detached language of those who accept a single truth. Both Merteuil and Valmont are interested in power, of course. But in the opening letters of the novel they at least pretend to have transcended the desire to exercise power over one another. Although Valmont might remember nostalgically a time when Merteuil "favoured me with sweeter names" (IV), he quickly puts this memory behind him. "But larger concerns demand our attention," he writes to her, for "conquest is our destiny" (IV). Theirs is the desire of theorists to exercise a mastery over the system they understand so thoroughly, and in their projects they pursue this end without, apparently, any defining reference to one another. They write only to make practical reciprocal requests and to compare notes the way cooperative scientists might.

The truth of their understanding not only makes Merteuil and Valmont equal. They also believe it makes them independent, self-sufficient, and self-defining. But the real strength of this self-sufficiency is tested at the very beginning of the novel by Valmont's attraction to Tourvel. This attraction marks the appearance of a predisposition for the thoroughly naive in the heart of a thoroughly sophisticated libertine. Valmont's other affairs may be trivial, mere exercises to prove his mastery. But his affair with Tourvel is a love story. It is the expression of a desire which is beyond the limits of the understanding he shares with Merteuil and, as such, will inevitably compromise this understanding.

"Let us be frank," Valmont writes to Merteuil early in the novel. "Since our intimacies are as cold as they are shallow, what we call happiness is scarcely even a pleasure. But shall I tell you something? I thought my heart had withered away, and, finding nothing left to me but my senses, I lamented my premature old age. Madame de Tourvel has restored the charming illusions of my youth. When I am with her, I have no need of pleasure to be happy" (VI). These illusions are obviously the illusions of love. What, exactly, are they?

Merteuil, we recall, discusses at some length the nature of love and its relation to pleasure. "Pleasure," she writes, "is the sole motive force behind the union of the sexes, [but it] is nevertheless not enough to form a bond between them" (CXXXI). Pleasure here is clearly the dissolution of orgasm, that "absolute self-abandon, that ecstasy of the senses, when pleasure is purified in its own excess" (V). This dissolution negates the distance between a man and a woman, but because it is immediately followed by the "disgust which repels" (CXXXI), it does so only momentarily.

In Merteuil's analysis love appears as both an extension and a transcendence of pleasure. Initially it strikes with an overpowering physical effect which drives lovers to give themselves to one another in the moment of pleasure. But love promises a bond between the sexes because it suspends the withdrawal which follows the experience of orgasm. Love allows the intensity of sensation to infuse the distance between the sexes, to make this distance resonant with the immediacy of the physical. Valmont has a vision of this when, soon after meeting Tourvel, he writes that "when I am with her, I have no need of pleasure to be happy" (VI). In the period immediately after she surrenders herself to Valmont, they seem actually to have reached this state. Valmont describes Tourvel during this period as someone "whose emotions, far from following the usual course, reached her senses through her heart; whom I have, for example, seen (and I don't refer to the first occasion) emerge from pleasure dissolved in tears, yet find it again in the first word that touched her sympathies" (CXXXIII).

To live so that a word has the force of a touch, Valmont must give himself to Tourvel. Again, apparently, he must sacrifice the authority which is the conventional prerogative of the man and recognize the arbitrary nature of his difference from her. But with Tourvel he surrenders this in order to accept the sensitivity and sensibility of the woman as a natural principle of feeling which, presumably, exists "beneath" the artifices of the conventional world. If Valmont accepts the feminine in himself, if he images and reflects her surrender, then he will discover a natural equality with her.

The medium and expression of this equality is not the analytical language Valmont uses with Merteuil but the expressive language of those whose hearts are in their mouths and whose words perfectly express their feelings. At those moments when he does give himself to Tourvel, Valmont finds himself speaking this language. "Intoxication was complete and reciprocal," he says of his first possession of Tourvel "and, for the first time with me, outlasted pleasure. I left her arms only to fall at her feet and swear eternal love; and, to tell the whole truth, I meant what I said" (CXXV). And when she hears it, Tourvel finally accepts and understands Valmont. "I admit I once found in him a certain deliberation, a reserve, which rarely left him, and which often reminded me, in spite of myself, of the false and cruel impression I had been given of him at first. But since he has been able to give himself up without restraint to the impulses of his heart, he seems to divine all the wishes of my own" (CXXXII).

Valmont and Tourvel/Valmont and Merteuil: In both relationships seduction becomes a search to discover a perfect understanding. With Valmont and Tourvel it is the natural conversation of lovers whose identity with one another leaves no room
for difference. With Valmont and Merteuil it is the conversation
of two absolutely free individuals whose independence from one
another makes their difference irrelevant and trivial. In the first
instance the two lovers work against the conventional opposition
of the sexes in order to reveal the "inherent" identity of male and
female in their common capacity to feel. In the second the two
friends assume the freedom to create themselves outside a conventional relationship, where men and women are, finally, dependent on one another because they can only define themselves in
terms of their difference.

In both cases understanding can exist only where difference is
eliminated and equality established in its place. The demand for
an equality of understanding in *Les Liaisons dangereuses* is the
need to speak to another with the clarity of intention that we
hear when we speak to ourselves. It is the desire for a perfect
coincidence of the self with another who is, in fact, no longer
other, whose understanding is so complete that one finds in them
only one's own idea of oneself. In the reciprocity of love
Valmont's "heart" reflects "the wishes of [Tourvel's] own"
(CXXXII). They are like two identical images which, when jux-
taposed, form one figure. In the equality of their friendship Valmont and Merteuil share "the same ideas, the same point of view"
(CXV). The "frankness and freedom" of their "long and perfect" conversation is free of the "insipid flattery" (CXXIX) that
characterizes the ordinary desires of men and women for one
another. They find here the confirmation of their own sense of
independence, the reflection of their own feeling of self-sufficiency. The dreams of love and friendship in this novel are essentially symmetrical visions of a state in which we have rescued
ourselves from the differences of the world and find ourselves,
at last, in one place. The lure of seduction is, finally, the possibility of finding or creating such an equality in the midst of difference.

To love a member of the opposite sex, as Valmont does Tourvel, or to be friends with a member of that sex, as he is with

Merteuil, is to believe in some way that either the clarity of intellect or the force of nature can generate a conversation which is free of difference. But we can see in *Les Liaisons dangereuses* how fragile either conversation is and how difficult it will be to hear the language of equality in the midst of the continual argument between men and women. Valmont and Merteuil *understand*, but their understanding expresses itself in a desire for conquest, a desire to master and define, which is only the conventional masculine attitude. Their difference is that they *do* understand and, consequently, they see each other as ironic masters rather than naive ones. But this is a distinction it would be easy to miss. Merteuil frequently reacts against Valmont's arrogance toward other women as if she fears it might possibly include her, making their friendship only a filmsy disguise for something much more common. At these times she seems unable to hear the ironic tone in his letters.

But it is also possible to lose the ability to hear this tone in our own voices. At these moments we become the stereotype instead of a self-conscious play on it. We become caught up in the conventional image of ourselves which the situation offers, and our irony becomes a cynicism which allows us to accept these traditional prerogatives. In this way Valmont might be very sincere when he surrenders himself to his feelings for Tourvel and accepts her surrender in return. But this surrender constantly offers him a seductive image of himself as the subtle libertine pretending love in order to possess and ruin.

From a certain point of view the ideals of love and friendship simply describe the opposition between masculine and feminine which they pretend to escape. Each attitude, in other words, is subject to becoming its conventional double. The question of an equality of understanding in either sense is really a question of the ability of these conversations to maintain themselves against the gravity of conventional discourse, which always works to make us hear in the tone of our friend or lover only the familiar but unpleasant voice of our opposite. The plot of *Les Liaisons dangereuses*—the rivalry which develops between Merteuil and Valmont over his affair with Tourvel and eventually consumes all the participants—answers this question by showing the persistent ability of convention to reappropriate the agreements of

love and understanding on its own terms and to make their conversations its own.

This process begins the very moment Valmont surrenders himself to his love for Tourvel. The letter he writes at this point, as
we have seen, describes the "complete and reciprocal" (CXXV)
intoxication which they share. But there is something immediately disturbing in the very existence of this letter. He claims to
have found in Tourvel an ecstatic presence which is the natural
end of desire. Yet he continues to write to Merteuil and to remain
implicated in the whole dialectic of their relationship. In this
sense the content of his letter, which in this passage insists on the
completeness of his experience, and the fact of the letter's existence, which implies the continuing desire for another form of
recognition, are incompatible.

In a paragraph, earlier in this same letter, which explicates this
contradiction, Valmont had described his seduction of Tourvel
from another point of view. "The excess of pleasure which I experienced in the amount of triumph," he writes, "and which I
still feel, is nothing but the delicious sensation of glory. I encourage myself in this belief because it spares me the humiliation of
thinking that I might have been dependent on the very slave I
had subjected to my will; that I might not find in myself alone
everything I require for my happiness; and that the capacity to
give me enjoyment of it in all its intensity might be the prerogative of any one woman to the exclusion of all others" (CXXV).
Here, in an entirely traditional manner, Valmont reserves the
experience of ecstasy or plentiude for himself and denies that it
is a product of his relation to Tourvel. She slaves for his pleasure,
which becomes simply the sign of his power and glory.

Valmont is being contradictory, of course. He is being both
the lover and the libertine. But this is his right. In *Les Liaisons
dangereuses* men are free to change their minds, to love in order
to experience love as possession and conquest, while for women
it means only ruin. What seems clear in Valmont's gradual adop-
tion of this conventional attitude is the failure of the reciprocity of
love to maintain itself against the attraction of a commonplace
image of masculine power. Behind this failure we can see that
here even the most intense sensation is not experienced as a meaning, a natural significance, which can express itself independently.

Whatever Valmont feels at the time, as soon as he records the experience he finds himself writing from the point of view of the libertine. The "excess of pleasure" becomes "the delicious sensation of glory" (CXXV). Pleasure does not extend itself into language but is, instead, displaced into it and defined by it. When Valmont writes of his sensations, he, too, is displaced and becomes their conventional meaning. He finds himself in his difference from Tourvel.

In this moment we can see the sense in Merteuil's attack on the two most common types of the feminine personality, namely, women of feeling or pleasure and women of sentiment. Her comments are obviously aimed at Cécile Volanges and Tourvel—the former a machine for pleasure, the latter a paragon of emotional intensity. But they are motivated by a more fundamental sense of the impossibility of women speaking directly to men through an appeal to some level of natural sexuality or sensitivity they might have in common. While this attempt seems to address a shared identity outside their difference, in reality it simply reinforces the conventional identification of the feminine and the "natural" experience of feeling and pleasure. Consequently this shared experience will always be recovered, talked about, within the context of the traditional opposition between the sexes. Its meaning will be defined by this difference just as the meaning of Valmont's night with Tourvel becomes power for the one and ruin for the other.

This would seem to authenticate Merteuil's own choice for the self-sufficiency which comes with an illusion-free wisdom. But Valmont's seduction of Tourvel corrupts his friendship with Merteuil in an interesting way. When he assimilates the intensity of orgasm to the abstract pleasures of triumph and assumes the traditional prerogatives of the man, he assumes these prerogatives as if they were the expression of an actual omnipotence. This is, finally, the effect of their very intensity, which, instead of carrying him "beyond" convention, seems to unquestionably validate and "naturalize" this power. His affair with Tourvel is no longer an experiment in the manipulation of signs but rather a clichéd seduction in which the woman is sacrificed in order to certify the man's power. So when Valmont returns to Merteuil in order to claim possession of her as a reward for his sacrifice of Tourvel, he comes not as an equal but as a man demanding his rights over a woman. The ironic distance which, within the context of his friendship with Merteuil, Valmont maintained toward his own masculinity has disappeared. He no longer offers Merteuil the equality of his friendship but the demeaning position of "a submissive slave" (CXXVII).

This transformation is clear when Valmont arrives at Merteuil's residence believing that she has agreed to his demands. Instead she has arranged for him to discover her with Cécile's lover, Danceny. Here Valmont becomes that least ironic of figures, the jealous husband. "Do you know, Vicomte, why I never married again," she confides to Valmont in response to his anger over this incident, "it was solely so that no one should have the right to object to anything I might do . . . And here you are writing me the most connubial letters possible! You speak of nothing but wrongs on my part and favours on yours! How can one fall short in the eyes of someone to whom one owes nothing? I cannot begin to imagine!" (CLII)

Merteuil reaffirms her essential independence in the face of a Valmont who has become only another version of Prévan. She assumes that her understanding will allow her to define herself even without the cooperation of Valmont. The war that develops between an ironic Merteuil and a Valmont who has simultaneously become the most jealous of husbands and the most demanding of lovers bears directly on this assumption. He now approaches as a representative of conventional relations between the sexes, challenging her claims to speak herself ironically. It is significant that this moment in which Valmont adopts the most traditional of attitudes is also the moment he is able to oppose her most effectively. In the letter he writes to her after he has discovered her with Danceny, he offers her only two possibilities: "I can leave the choice to you, but I cannot remain in uncertainty" (CLIII). Between the alternatives of a renewed sexual intimacy and an enmity which can only lead to their mutual ruin there are, he continues, "a thousand others we might take" (CLIII). But Valmont rejects any but the most clearly defined choices and demands the most unequivocal of answers. "The reply I ask for does not require long and beautiful sentences," he concludes. "A word will suffice" (CLIII).

Valmont forces Merteuil to choose between the two alternatives traditionally open to women, namely, enslavement or ruin. His ability to foist this choice upon her says something about the attempt by women like Merteuil—who, for one reason or another, have been denied the explicit enjoyment of power within a system—to redefine their conventionally inferior position as a strong one through a certain theoretical analysis and understanding of the basis of power itself. Again, the effectiveness of this attempt lies in the assumption that this analysis allows one to transcend a naive belief in the reality of the masculine. This understanding, then, is returned as an ability to employ power more effectively because its arbitrary nature is recognized and accepted. Such manipulation takes its meaning and pleasure from its own effectiveness rather than a mystical belief in its own reality or in the inherent value of the objects it seeks to possess. This is why it seems so self-contained, so independent, and why Merteuil seems so self-defining.

But if we consider Merteuil's attitude toward the incident with Prévan, we see that this is really not the case. The point of the incident—and the pleasure and significance which she finds in it—does not lie in the actual ruin of Prévan but in the ironic reversal of her feminine role, which is affected by his disgrace. This is a meaning which her victim perceives dimly if at all. It exists, in effect, in her narration to Valmont and his reading of the true intention of her actions. Merteuil's letter to Valmont is not a cold and "scientific" account of her adventure, given more or less after the fact. It is preening, self-congratulatory, narcissistic, and charged with an intense erotic quality. "How lucky you are to have me for a friend," she writes in the third paragraph of this letter." When you have to remove a formidable opponent [Prévan] from the lists, it is again I you invoke in your prayers, and I who fulfill your wishes. Indeed, if you do not spend the rest of your life giving me thanks I shall think you ungrateful" (LXXXV). Merteuil demands Valmont's recognition of her omnipotence, which will exist for her only when he accepts and returns it. The intensity with which Merteuil turns to Valmont for the recognition that will complete her conquest reveals that for Laclos the pleasures of a detached exercise of power have no more inherent meaning than the immediate pleasure of sexuality. They exist only when they are communicated to someone who hears and understands.

Once they are communicated in this way, of course, they become implicated again in the whole system of conventional differences which structures the relation between speaker and listener, masculine and feminine. Merteuil's position is an example of the way an explicit demystification of the basis of power and meaning can easily become the very error which it denounces. She could silently exercise power and manipulate her world independently. But her real desire is to be recognized as powerful, and for this she is as dependent on Valmont for her pleasure as the most stupid woman in her world, who unquestioningly accepts the belief that her man is the source of her feeling and sensation. Her pretensions to independence, then, are only a particularly effective kind of facade designed to seduce and fascinate Valmont, who inspired in her "the only one of my desires that has even for a moment gained sway over me" (LXXXI). Her philosophy is simply clarity in the service of illusion.

Merteuil, in constituting herself as an ironic reversal of the feminine, had defined herself as a certain ambiguous play within a system of fixed meanings, a certain tonality which signals this reversal, a pun. This meaning existed, could see itself as free and self-defining, only as long as Valmont allowed this tonality to exist and responded to it. When he denies her the ambiguity necessary for this play, he reveals that her freedom is only an illusion maintained in the midst of an actual, completely conventional dependence.

When Merteuil rejects Valmont, the reality of her dependence becomes clear. At the end of the novel, after he has made her correspondence with him public, she finds herself defined by both forces she had initially suppressed: by a physicality which now asserts itself in terms of disease and mutilation, and by a conventionality which makes her an icon of the ruined woman. Merteuil's fate is particularly violent and grotesque. But this seems to testify to the intense hostility which convention directs against any attempt to redefine the feminine as a position of mastery. Conventional morality will tolerate the ambivalence of seduction as it is played out by men because here the ironic suspension of masculinity vis-à-vis the woman manifests itself, finally, as a renewed insistence on the traditional position of the male. Valmont becomes the romantic slave of Tourvel only to reassert himself more forcefully as her master. In the case of Merteuil, however, the attempt to make the feminine the target of irony and enact it as a position of masculine power has an altogether different effect. Merteuil's success would reveal that the assignment of qualities of masculine power and feminine sensitivity to the male and female, respectively, is only conventional. The recognition of her power would involve an impossible public recognition by convention of its own arbitrary nature.

*Les Liaisons dangereuses* can be read in this way as a study of the frustration of our desire to understand and be understood, which is, finally, the intent of seduction in this novel. In each case failure occurs at the precise moment when these characters try to act on this understanding, incorporate it into their lives, and experience it as a situation beyond difference. Valmont sees in Tourvel an image of the lost illusions and intensities of his youth. Yet when he surrenders the reserve which marks his difference from her and gives himself to their equality, he only reaffirms that he is her master. Merteuil sees in Valmont the reflection of her own self-sufficient understanding. Yet the moment she tries to separate herself from him and experience their equality as her independence, she finds herself subject again to male authority.

In these instances we can see that the idea of equality describes the inherently contradictory situation of "individuals." On the one hand, equality implies independence, a desire to somehow marry their vision of themselves, to become autonomous, their own source, the author of their own lives. On the other hand, equality presents independence as a condition which is always established in relation to an other, the other with whom one wants to be equal. Tourvel and Valmont try to escape this contradiction in their identification with one another. This is the dream of love. Valmont and Merteuil try to escape it by understanding and rising above their defining relation to one another. This is the illusion of theory. From this point of view Laclos shows clearly that the desire for equality can never be anything but a dream of autonomy staged in the context of an actual dependence.

Individuals will be defined by their difference from one another, a difference which ultimately will be read in the context of the conventional meanings within which they exist. It is no accident that Valmont and Merteuil have the power to ruin one another and that this power rests, finally, in their ability to expose one another to the moral judgment of society. The force of this argument bears directly on those who, like Valmont and Tourvel, succumb to the illusion that some natural equality exists beneath the artificial distinctions of society. But it also applies to those, like Merteuil, who believe that because these distinctions are only arbitrary and have no natural validity, they can be manipulated and redefined easily in order to create this equality.

The project of seduction, then, is ultimately subject to convention. The authority of convention expresses itself most clearly in the power of gossip. Gossip does not see either nature or intention. Its ability to define meaning is precisely the ability of any system of convention to define without regard to any idea of an inherent meaning or origin. When Merteuil schemes to make Gercourt the "laughing-stock of Paris" (II) or plans to publish Valmont's memoirs for her glory, she intends to assume this power for herself and make it speak for her. The publication of *Les Liaisons dangereuses* fulfills Merteuil's vision, but it does so in a way that demonstrates clearly her failure to master this language. It is gossip which reasserts the difference between the sexes and makes her that most clichéd figure, the fallen woman.

In this sense *Les Liaisons dangereuses* circulates as a form of gossip. It seems to invite our moralistic response and to express this response in the way we do when we gossip. Gossip is never the product of a personal judgment. People who gossip speak with the voice of the system, and in their pronouncements they enact its differences. When we read the novel we are the other who reads Merteuil, the place originally occupied by Valmont. The moralistic reader who smiles approvingly at Merteuil's disfigurement reveals how impotent intention is against a reader who will never understand and sympathize, who instead replies in the impersonal voice of gossip, the voice of a system which will always have the last word and will always impose on the individual some uncomfortable difference.

But this will be true not only of overtly moralistic readings of the novel but also of those "philosophic" readings which would emphasize the "failure" of Valmont and Merteuil. These readers, too, will click their tongue knowingly at those foolish enough to attempt to realize their ideas or their feelings. *Les Liaisons dangereuses* has a curious and disturbing way of presenting the most sophisticated points of view as mirror images of the least sophisticated, of establishing a resemblance which shows that the first are only versions of the second. So the most conscious seduction becomes a love affair; the distanced friendship of Valmont and Merteuil is transformed into a bad marriage. The novel is about the impossibility of ever totally escaping those forces which fashion us and our world as stereotypes. And this is nowhere more true than in the way Laclos's novel tempts us to celebrate the ruin of Valmont and Merteuil and, with it, the destruction of the self. At this point our philosophic wisdom becomes only a reflection of the truth of the village gossip. We try to master the failure of ironic understanding by becoming ironic about irony itself and are forced to live this "wisdom" as an uncomfortable cynicism which accepts the passionless conventionality of Mme. de Volanges or Mme. de Rosemonde because it sees no alternative and rejoices in the misfortunes of others because they seem to confirm this acceptance.[8]

But it would be a mistake to read the novel in such a narrow way. *Les Liaisons dangereuses* does not deny the existence of moments of sexuality, feeling, or understanding by showing that they are illusions. The novel's point, really, is that these moments do exist within the system of conventionality. It simply denies them the power to fully realize themselves by establishing either an absolute control of meaning or some continuous relationship with the "natural." Such moments, in other words, do not describe positions of undetermined reflexion or natural sexuality around which an independent subjectivity could constitute itself. They exist in a necessary, dialectical relationship with convention in a way that determines the limits and the trajectory of projects such as Valmont's and Merteuil's. These will always find themselves reabsorbed, redefined within the conventional. But, by the same token, convention cannot completely suppress either sexuality or the play of irony. These exist as limited moments—but ones which persistently appear. The libertine world is formed by

the intersection of a pure and passionless conventionality, represented by Mme. de Volanges or Mme. de Rosemonde, and a desire which, in its extreme form, produces a Merteuil or a
Valmont. In it seduction is always being demystified, convention-
alized, suppressed. But it is also constantly being provoked; Merteuil's revolt is generated by the harsh and arbitrary definition of
women and Valmont's love is prompted by the cold and shallow
intimacies allowed by convention.[9]

This line of reasoning leads us inevitably to the meaning of the
editorial apparatus which stands between the reader and the body
of letters. It consists of a short "Note from the Publisher" and a
somewhat longer "Preface by the Editor," in which he explains
his role in assembling the manuscript. As cursory as these seem to
be, they occupy an important place in the novel. Needless to say,
editorship in *Les Liaisons dangereuses* can never be innocent. An
editor supplies a context which determines how a text will circulate and be read. His power over a manuscript is precisely the
power to transpose, displace, and redefine which, for Merteuil,
constitutes the function of authorship. The last seduction in *Les
Liaisons dangereuses* takes place here, in the relationship which
the editor establishes between himself and his text and, through
this text, with the object of his seduction—the reader. It is here,
then, that the novel makes its final statement on the project of individuality.[10]

An initial reading of the editor's preface (EP), however, seems
only to emphasize his transparent conventionality. He presents
himself as a passive agent who has merely made the letters available to the public. These, he says, are a collection rather than a
novel. He has merely added a few brief notes.

There is, however, one aspect of the letters which he has wanted
to alter. All of them are characterized by errors of style or diction. There is not one of the correspondents, he writes, "who had
not committed the grossest errors, which could not fail to meet
with criticism" (EP). The editor has wanted to anticipate this
criticism and make further corrections concerned with the "purity of diction and style" (EP). His intentions here are, like his
restraint, a measure of his conventionality. He wants to act as the
agent of stylistic rectitude and suppress the scandal of error. His
manipulation of the text would not make it his own and give it

his meaning. He would regularize it and eliminate those errors which are the very mark of individuality of the correspondents.

The editor has been prevented from doing this by the owners of the letters. They argue that "every reasonable reader would surely expect to find mistakes in a collection of letters that had passed between private individuals, since of all those letters published hitherto by various authors of reputation (including certain Academicians) not one could be found totally beyond reproach in this respect" (EP). Consequently, "it would have been as much counter to probability as to truth if the eight to ten persons participating in this correspondence had written with equal correctness" (EP). This assertion that the realism of the letters demands the retention of errors reminds us again of the continued persistence of variety within the seemingly omnipotent power of convention to standardize. Error here is the companion of authorship. By implication, it is the sign of an idiosyncratic desire in language, of the inevitable need to speak personally and, consequently, to deviate from the purely conventional; it is the need to be understood by another and to find in that understanding both your meaning and your satisfaction.

To speak with the voice of convention would be to speak without error, impersonally, without an individual passion. In *Les Liaisons dangereuses* this transcendence of desire is possible only for elderly women. The fact that even academicians cannot attain it undercuts the editor's initial pretensions to transparency. But this is clear in the very existence of the editor's preface, which testifies to his need to address the reader personally, to stage himself in the text as a meaning, to seek the reader's understanding.

The awareness of the editor's personal address leads to an ironic reading of his disclaimer of authorship, a reading which would place it within the tradition of such prefaces in eighteenth-century novels. The publisher's note (PN) to the novel invites such a reading when it warns us that the collection is, in fact, "a novel" (PN) and alerts us to the extensive changes which the editor has, in fact, made in the text. From this point of view the publisher clearly seems to be only a version of the editor, he writes to alert the careful reader to the ironic meaning of the editor's apparent passivity. The author is simply diverting and redefining the conventional relationship between editor and text in such a way that it becomes, in fact, the sign of authorship, the locus of a controlling interpretation.

The interplay between the publisher's note and the editor's preface invites us to search for this meaning and find the novel's significance in an authorial intention which is hidden behind this conventional surface. Readers who accept this invitation finds themselves drawn into a relationship with the author which is curiously similar to the friendship between Merteuil and Valmont. This, too, is the result of a mutual seduction based on the one's ability to read the ironic meaning of the other. In his note the publisher insists that the events and the characters in the novel could not exist in contemporary Paris. The author, he says, "has evidently been seduced [*séduit*] by hopes of attracting more interest for his story into locating it in his own time and country— we consider him very much to blame for venturing to represent, under the guise of our costume and our customs, a way of life so altogether alien to us" (PN). Like Merteuil the author conceals a strange and "alien" vision within the "costume and customs" of ordinary life in the hope of finding a reader, like Valmont, who will penetrate this disguise and understand him. The vision of an understanding reader who will see the unifying intent existing behind the incongruities and inconsistencies of the text allows the author to see himself as a unity existing behind the apparent diversity of voices in the work.

On the other hand, readers confronted by this variety of styles and errors in the novel will look for their source in a single figure. Speaking again of the mistakes which riddle the manuscript, the editor remarks that "the general run of readers, seduced by the idea that everything that is printed is the result of deliberation, will think they detect in others the labored manners of an author who appears in person behind the characters through whom he speaks" (EP). Errors here become the sign of a controlling intentionality behind the work, the mark of a unity which is the sum of their limited particularity. Readers are drawn to interpret these signs by their desire for this figure of mastery and control who is the author. From this point of view expression and interpretation are complementary movements of desire which hope to establish the equality of understanding between author and reader which is the dream of seduction. Each finds in the imagined wholeness of the other a locus from which their errors, the momentary and partial deviations form convention which are their individuality, appear as the consistent manifestation of a single personality which exists "behind" its manifestations.

Here the editor's position has apparently been redefined. He is no longer the passive agent of convention forced against his will to tolerate error. Instead, like Merteuil he has transformed this position, appropriated it for his own personal use. Errors, in turn, are no longer trivial, partial, or occasional but collectively reflect a whole person who exists within, but is in no sense limited or defined by, his conventional disguise.

The editor, however, is quick to warn us against the seductive danger of this approach. His comments on the general reader's desire for such a figure occurs in a passage in which he lists reasons why his readers will be dissatisfied with his work. "This collection," he warns us, "can please very few. Libertines of either sex will find it in their interest to decry a book which may do them harm . . . Would-be free-thinkers will not be interested in a devout woman, who, because she is devout, they will regard as a ninny . . . From another point of view, readers of fastidious taste will be disgusted at the excessively simple and incorrect style of many of these letters" (EP).

The general reader's search for a masterful author, then, is presented as only one of a number of approaches to the work, each of which is only the expression of that reader's opinions and desires. It is not a privileged method which establishes the "real" meaning of the work but only one prejudice among many. Reading here does not produce—cannot produce—a total coincidence of author and reader, intent and response. Instead it fragments the work. The author will never be able to find himself in a coherent reading. He will see himself broken, dispersed, and partially reflected in his readers' responses in a way which can never be consolidated into one unified reflection of his message. By the same token, no single reader will ever be able to find his or her image hidden in the work. The novel will always seem inconsistent and fragmentary.

The readers who work to construct the figure of the author as a double whose power of expression and control matches and

confirms their skill at interpretation will find in the "labored manner" (EP) of this construct only the reflection of their own un-
successful efforts and will leave the work, at best, only partially
satisfied. The editor's almost paranoid concern with the unattrac-
tiveness of this work for his readers, then, is not "the false modesty of an author" (EP) but a recognition of his real limitations
and the resulting frustration of his readers. In an earlier passage
in his preface he addressed this issue in a more general context.
The success of a work, he tells us, is often the result of its choice
of subject, which is agreeable to the reader, rather than the way
the subject is treated. He then states:

> Now, since this collection contains, as its title announces, the
> letters of a whole section of society, a diversity of interests is
> represented which are not all those of the reader. Moreover, since
> nearly all the sentiments expressed are either pretended or dis-
> sembled, they can excite only the interest of curiosity, an interest
> always much inferior to that of feeling; one, above all, which, in-
> clining the reader less to indulgence, leaves errors of detail more
> open to criticism, since it is they that continually frustrate the one
> desire he wishes to satisfy. (EP)

The issue in this passage has to do with the diversity of readers
and subjects. The success of a work depends on an identity between reader and subject matter which permits the pleasure of
identification, sympathy, and "feeling." But since this work does
present a diversity of styles and subjects, no single reader will be
able to find him or herself in the totality of the work. Consequently readers will, for the most part, be limited to the "inferior" enjoyment of curiosity, the detached interest one gives to
that which is different or other. Since difference does frustrate
"the one desire he wishes to satisfy" because it does not allow the
reader's imaginary identification with the subject, curiosity will
always be experienced as a kind of dissatisfaction which leaves
readers aware of the work's "errors of detail."

In this passage the editor abandons any pretensions to an absolute mastery, to an ability to make himself understood in a way
that would establish a common agreement between himself and
his readers. But since errors are inevitable and cannot be eliminated, this obviously does not mean a return to a passive and in-

nocent conventionality. He locates himself in a space between the two which, finally, can only be the space of error.

The "author," then, is fashioned out of the impossibility, on the one hand, of speaking, acting, or writing with absolute fastidiousness and rectitude, and the impossibility, on the other, of ever totally integrating these errors, making them the consistent expression of an intention which can be fully read and understood by others. Error signals the randomness and inconsistency of human personality. Of course, this is true not only of the editor himself but also of his readers, who are characterized not by the uniformity of the desires and prejudices they bring to the work but by their diversity.

Error describes not only our own deviation from convention but also our difference from one another in the individuality and diversity of our errors. Consequently we will always mistake one another, find our understanding limited by the difference in our errors. Our relation to one another will be like our relation to the editor's work. For the most part we will find in others only the "inferior" pleasures of curiosity, and this will be broken only occasionally by moments of sympathy and understanding which can never be extended to form a total, comprehensive image of the other. The "person" will always be read like a misspelled word which marks an individuality without actually expressing it, or like a connotation which suggests a personal meaning but will never be as stable and explicit as denotation.

From this point of view we might say about one another what the editor says about the diversity of his work: We offer one another a "variety of styles" which succeed in sparing us "the tedium, at least, of uniformity" (EP). Yet despite the editor's acceptance of the inevitability of the differences which will separate himself and his readers, the tone of his preface is not that of the philosopher who can speak only out of a detached curiosity. Although he says he is "still very far from expecting any success," he confesses, "I must declare, with the same candor, that, if this collection had not seemed to me worthy of being offered to the public, I should have nothing to do with it" (EP). The editor, in other words, does not trivialize and surrender the activity of expression but only the dream of finding his meaning realized and reflected in a reader who understands and agrees completely. He accepts the frustration of this demand, yet he commits himself to his desire to publish and continues to address his readers across their differences.

The editor abandons the pretensions of authorship, but he does seem to locate a conversation between the reader and the author which is neither some version of the dream of equality nor simply the exchange of two fundamentally uninterested parties who are merely passing time. This conversation can only be the quarrel which occurs between those who do not agree with one another. The interplay between the publisher's note and the editor's preface is designed, finally, to provoke this argument. It presents the editor as someone who, though he is not in control of the work, is somehow responsible for its errors and inadequacies. He is the person to whom you can address your complaints and who invites disagreement.

Readers who accept his invitation will no longer expect to find themselves reflected in the image of a coherent author, just as the editor no longer expects to encounter an understanding reader. These readers, after all, have been warned that this figure does not exist. But those who love the novel and persist in reading and interpreting it will find the editor in this ambiguous presence, someone who is at once nowhere and everywhere, blameless yet responsible. They will find him, in other words, in the way his work resists and frustrates them. The opposition between reader and editor will never be concluded or resolved in a moment when they agree and understand each other. But in their frustration they provoke one another into a conversation which, like all deeply felt antagonism, is close, personal, and intimate.

The chapter which follows is a reading of the comedies of William Congreve. In these plays the lover and the woman confront one another in a by now all too familiar situation and follow a by now all too familiar course. In Congreve the heroines, like Mme. de Merteuil, define themselves by their detached understanding of the arbitrary nature of sexual difference. Consequently they, too, hold themselves aloof from any surrender to the pleasure of feeling, which would be read as a "natural" susceptibility to emotion and would allow the world to define them as just another woman. It is the men in Congreve's plays who must accept the burden of loving. Like Valmont, these are all men of the world who turn from the game of seduction in order to pursue the women of their choice with all the intensity of the truly naive. They speak, in other words, for the persistence of desire in the face of experience and for its specificity, for its insistence on choosing its object according to its own criteria rather than according to conventional wisdom.

Congreve, too, sets these two positions against one another, allows each to demystify the pretensions of the other, and shows how both the intensity of the lover and the detachment of the woman are motivated by the same vision of a response which coincides perfectly with the speaker's questions. But Congreve is particularly interested in the way he is able to move beyond this moment of demystification. Like the fictional editor in Laclos, Congreve is more interested in the lessons of this argument than he is in simply explicating the impossibility of its complete resolution. The most interesting of the couples in his plays finally accept one another when they discover, paradoxically, that to love the other is to argue with that which, in its difference, can never agree but only misunderstand.

# V

# William Congreve and
# the Conversation of Opposites

THE COUPLES WHO ARE at the center of Congreve's comedies—
Vainlove and Araminta, Mellefont and Cynthia, Valentine and
Angelica, Mirabell and Millamant—are at once the most attractive
and the most disturbing figures in his plays. They are attractive,
of course, because they are unique. In their world the difference
between intelligence and stupidity is the difference between the
characters of Tattle and Scandal in *Love for Love*. The first is a
manipulative fop who hoards the reputations of women he has
seduced. The second is a manipulative wit who follows the same
course but accomplishes it in a more acceptable style. This is a
real difference, to be sure, and an important one for Congreve.
But the area it circumscribes is a little too narrow to be anything
but claustrophobic.

Alone among their contemporaries, these couples seem to be
able to conceive of themselves in different—larger—terms, to imagine a joy which is not merely a pleasure and a happiness which is
not merely the choice of resignation over frustration. In this way
they attract all our own romantic longings to live a life which is
fuller, more intense, and more brightly colored than our ordinary
surroundings.

These couples are disturbing, however, because although they
are each clearly separate from their surroundings, they are not
so clearly together in their distinctiveness. These couples fall naturally into the attitudes of romantic love in which the intense

lover contemplates the reluctant woman. But in their case the opposition of distance and desire is played out in the paradox of the argument: an intimate conversation about—and over—difference. This argument troubles us because it calls into question the real possibility of their love; it disturbs our reassuring identification with their uniqueness and threatens to offer us only the choice between Tattle and Scandal. In this sense their fate is ours, and the suspense of these plays comes from our uncertainty about the terms on which their argument will be resolved—or, in fact, if it will be resolved at all.

The theme of Congreve's plays can, of course, be formulated in a number of ways: the conflict between love and society; the opposition of providence and chance.[1] But it is clear that one way to question these works would be to ask about the terms of this argument. What is the nature of the mark which sets both the lover and the woman apart from their world but against each other? In what way can they be reconciled?

BELLMOUR: . . . Couldst thou be content to marry Araminta?
VAINLOVE: Could you be content to go to heaven?
. . . . . . . . . . . . . . . . . . . . . . . . . . . . . . . . . . . . . . . . . . . . . . . . . . . . . . . . . . .
BELLMOUR: But how the devil dost thou expect to get her if she never yield?
VAINLOVE: That's true; but I would—
BELLMOUR: Marry her without her consent; thou'rt a riddle beyond woman. (TOB, III, ii)[2]

MILLAMANT: Come, don't look grave then. Well, what do you say to me?
MIRABELL: I say that a man may as soon make a friend by his wit, or a fortune by his honesty, as win a woman by plain-dealing and sincerity.
MILLAMANT: Sententious Mirabell!—Prithee, don't look with that violent and inflexible wise face, like Solomon at the dividing of the child in an old tapestry hanging. (WW, II, ii)

VALENTINE: Nay, faith, now let us understand one another, hypocrisy apart.—The comedy draws toward an end, and let us think of leaving acting, and be ourselves; and since you have loved me, you must own, I have at length deserved you should confess it.
ANGELICA: (Sighs) I would I have loved you!—for Heaven knows I pity you. (LL, III, iii)

The heroes of Congreve's plays are the quintessential men of their world, the wittiest and most manipulative of their peers. Yet in their attitude toward the women they love they are distinguished precisely by their distance from the prevailing scepticism and self-interest of this world. They persist in their suits despite the advice of their friends, who urge the triviality of all women, the absolute reality of self-interest, and the impossibility of success.

The singularity of these lovers, their distinctiveness, is marked by the relative openness with which they express their feelings. Although none of Congreve's other lovers are as lavish in their display of affection as Valentine is in *Love for Love*, each of them could say, with Mirabell, that "for a discerning man" he was "somewhat too passionate a lover" (WW, I, ii). Valentine welcomes his illegitimate child by another woman while simultaneously waiting on Angelica and Mirabell schemes for a former mistress. Theirs is not the naive commitment of the inexperienced. Nevertheless, in a world where, to paraphrase Mme. de Merteuil in *Les Liaisons dangereuses*, to say "I love you" is to say "you own me," none of these men try to mask their feelings from the women they love by feigning interest in a rival. "What would you give that you could help loving me?" asks Millamant. "I would give something that you did not know I could not help it" (WW, II, ii), replies Mirabell. But Mirabell does not try to mislead Millamant by counterfeiting a renewed attraction to Mrs. Fainall.

In this way Congreve's lovers insist on their distinctiveness. Of course, other characters in these plays do fall in love: Mrs. Marwood with Mirabell; Sylvia with Vainlove; Lady Touchwood with Mellefont; and Maskwell with Cynthia. But while in these cases love is not simply the cynical disguise for a real desire for money or power, it expresses itself in a similar way as a demand for possession or revenge. It attempts to force a certain response.

Congreve's lovers, on the other hand, present themselves as men who are beyond this kind of calculation. They do not want to force a response. They want to receive one which is freely given. These men certify their acceptance of a woman's prerogative to surrender herself by their willingness to be passive, to undertake the risk of sentimentality, and to remain in various uncomfortable and ridiculous postures of anticipation while waiting for a word from the one woman who can release them.

The lover offers. He declares his love with all the honesty and sincerity at his disposal. To borrow a phrase from *Love for Love*, these men speak their mind and hope that the women they love will recognize this and respond in the same manner. In *Love for Love* Valentine's younger brother, Ben, returns from years at sea completely innocent of the manners and ambitions of polite society. This life gives him an independence from his father which allows him to express himself directly. "I love to speak my mind," he says to Mrs. Frail when the two are discussing his father's inevitable opposition to their marriage. "Father has nothing to do with me. Nay, I can't say that neither; he has something to do with me. But what does that signify? if so be, that I be'n't minded to be steered by him, tis as tho'f he should strive against wind and tide" (LL, III, iv). For Ben love is a natural force against which the structures of patriarchal society "signify" nothing. His speech can only be the direct expression of his desire. "To speak one thing and to think just the contrary way," he says, "is, as it were, to look one way and to row another" (LL, III, iii).

Ben's attitude is designed to contrast, in obvious and entirely stereotypical ways, with the language of a society in which, to borrow the words of another character in *Love for Love*, "lying is a figure of speech, that interlards the greatest part of . . . conversation" (LL, IV, iii).

Lying accounts for much of the brilliant linguistic surface of Congreve's plays. But if Congreve captures the gleam of this surface, his plays document the real terror and claustrophobic atmosphere that lies just beneath it. In *Love for Love* Mrs. Frail, "who has no great stock either of fortune or reputation" (LL, IV, ii), is in search of a husband and cannot afford to compromise herself in any way. Yet she has been seen riding in a coach in Covent Garden with a man. When her sister, Mrs. Foresight, corrects her, Mrs. Frail insists on the essential innocence of this encounter. "Lord," she says, "where's the comfort of this life, if we can't have the happiness of conversing where we like?" Her sister admits the probable innocence of this act. "But," she continues, "can't you converse at home? I own it, I think there is no happiness like conversing with an agreeable man; I don't quarrel with that, nor I don't think but your conversation was very innocent; but the place is public, and to be seen with a man in a hackney coach is scandalous: what if anybody else should have seen you alight, as I did?—How can anybody be happy, while they're in perpetual fear of being seen and censured?" (LL, II, ii)

Ben can speak freely because he has led a seafaring existence and is not concerned with economic gain or social position. But this exchange between Mrs. Foresight and Mrs. Frail illustrates the very different situation which exists in a world where the desire for money and status is primary and is continuously mediated through the conversation of others. The laws which govern this conversation, namely, the rules of decorum and convention, define without regard to what we think of as the intrinsic qualities of a person or act. When you live within the confines of these laws, you are denied the innocence of your immediate reactions and the experience of your life as the natural expression of your personal feelings. The reality of your actions will aways lie outside yourself in the anonymous others who gossip and judge.

The meaning of the conversation between Mrs. Frail and the man she rides with in the coach is not determined by the actual nature of their feelings or the words they exchange—however "innocent" or "guilty" these might, in fact, be—but by a judgment which is pronounced without regard to the content of this conversation. To protect themselves they must conceal or disguise their encounter, treat it as if it was, in fact, something else. Initially lying might seem an assertion of freedom, a way to exist on your own terms behind a screen of misrepresentation. But this incident allows us to see what is constrained and forced in such misrepresentation. Lying is never a completely free act. It always acknowledges the determining power of some law—decorum, financial necessity—to force a certain form of presentation. Lying is the experience of this dislocation, the experience of having to speak in a language not your own.

Ben, of course, is free of these constraints, bound neither by decorum nor by an interest in his father's estate. We are undoubtedly supposed to see a parallel between the independence of Ben and that of his brother, Valentine, who, to prove his love for Angelica, sacrifices his own fortune and, finally, the right to his inheritance. In his hatred of his son, Valentine's father, Sir

Sampson, is a representative of all these external factors which seek to constrain and displace natural desire, to force it to lie. He looks forward eagerly to his son's poverty and, particularly, to the way it will compel him to speak the language of economic necessity. "You shall see the rogue show himself, and make love to some desponding Cadua of four-score for sustenance. Odd, I love to see a young spendthrift forced to cling to an old woman for support, like ivy round a dead oak: faith I do; I love to see 'em hug and cotton together, like down upon a thistle" (LL, III, iii).

The power of love to speak directly, without constraint or regard to the conventions of society, is both its strength and its danger. In the second act of *The Double-Dealer* the villain, Mask-well, obsessed by his love for Cynthia, is on the point of betraying both his symbolic father, Lord Touchwood, and his friend, Mellefont. But he defends the apparent immorality of his acts.

> Cynthia, let thy beauty gild my crimes; and whatsoever I commit of treachery or deceit, shall be imputed to me as a merit.—Treachery! what treachery? love cancels all the bonds of friendship, and sets men right upon their first foundations.—Duty to kings, piety to parents, gratitude to benefactors and fidelity to friends, are different and particular ties: but the name of rival cuts 'em all asunder, and is a general acquittance. Rival is equal, and love like death, a universal leveller of mankind. (DD, II, i)

The association of love and incest runs throughout this play. Mellefont is accused at various times of making advances both to his aunt, Lady Touchwood, and to his prospective mother-in-law, Lady Plyant. Lady Touchwood is, in fact, in love with Mellefont and attempts to seduce him. Love is a force which is always on the point of violating the limits the social order has placed on desire. Love operates outside this system, establishing relations between individuals without regard to hierarchy, obligation, or the fixed order of generations.

But if Maskwell speaks for what is chaotic and destructive in love, Congreve's lovers speak for what seems positive. Precisely because love transcends convention it seems able to return men to "their first foundations" (DD, II, i), to return them to the naturalness and independence of Ben, and consequently to liberate them from the need to misrepresent their thoughts and actions. Behind the figure of the lover who speaks his mind, then, is some idea of love as natural desire untainted by the artificiality of conventional motives of economics and decorum. Love, if allowed to take its course, will find its natural end and satisfaction.

THE NATURAL OPENNESS OF CONGREVE'S LOVERS is, of course, met by the absolute refusal of Congreve's heroines to recognize and respond to the obvious sincerity of their lovers. At this point the lover's frustration is as infinite as his love.

Initially the silence of these heroines seems the result of their essentially conservative adherence to the artificial codes of society. In *Love for Love* Ben's father intends for him to marry Miss Prue, a young girl from the country who is in every way his equal in naiveté. Before the match can take place, however, she is corrupted by Tattle, who teaches her the rules governing conversation in polite society. When he asks her if she could love him, she replies with a simple "yes." You must lie, he corrects her, for "all well-bred persons lie.—Besides, you are a woman, you must never speak what you think." "Oh Lord," Prue replies, "I swear this is pure!—I like it better than our old-fashioned way of speaking one's mind" (LL, II, i).

This scene between Tattle and Prue not only emphasizes the artificial language of the well bred but also what seems to be the particular susceptibility of women to the attractions of this language. Ben maintains his integrity against the threats of his father and the seductive efforts of Mrs. Frail. Prue succumbs to an obvious fool. In this Prue would seem to be an ironic commentary on the maddening reticence of Congreve's heroines.

But there is an important difference between these heroines and other women for Congreve. In most cases a woman's reticence is a screen for indulgence. "Your words must contradict your thoughts," Tattle tells Prue, "but your actions may contradict your words" (LL, II, i). In the case of Congreve's heroines, however, this is not the case. They refuse all offers, all seductions with the same resolute offhandedness they display toward their lovers. Although these women could never be called naive, they retain an essential innocence. They are active and skilled participants in the gossip and raillery of their world. But they are never the subject or the victim of this gossip. They are involved in no schemes for profit, have no liaisons with other men, and have committed no indiscretions. In a world in which the physical desire of women is not only acknowledged but celebrated, they set themselves apart from the pervasive sexuality which surrounds them.

The consistent refusal of Congreve's heroines to respond to the desires of others is only an effect of the consistency with which they deny their own desires. Although privately Araminta might pray that "if love be the fever . . . kind heaven avert the cure" (TOB, II, ii), she will never accept this fever to the point where she will speak or act on it. Although Millamant might confess to herself that she loves Mirabell "violently" (WW, IV, i), she will never openly acknowledge these feelings. In Congreve's plays "to live" and "to desire" are synonymous; only his heroines deny this equation. In this refusal they have taken a vow as rigorous as any nun's. It is this vow which is behind their refusal to answer their lovers.

The woman's silence, then, is not simply a mindless act based convention or a trick of seduction. It questions the lover's devotion to his love and his acceptance of the apparent simplicity of his feelings. The argument between the lover and the woman is an argument about the nature of desire itself, in which the lover's absolute belief in the "natural" reality of his desire is opposed by the absolute scepticism of the woman not only toward his feelings but toward her own as well.

Why do Congreve's women deny their own feelings? There is nothing in the initial conflict of offer and refusal which provides an answer to this question. For some couples in these plays, moreover, their relationship never goes beyond the repetition of this initial moment. "I burn," Bellmour tells Belinda in *The Old Bachelor*. "O gad, I hate your hideous fancy!" she replies, adding "you said that once before.—If you must talk impertinently, for Heaven's sake let it be with variety; don't come always, like the devil, wrapped in flames" (TOB, II, ii). Lovers such as Bellmour attempt to "weary their women into a forgiveness" (TOB, V, ii). But on this level the love of the man is no match for the scepticism of the woman.

Most arguments, however, develop. Participants try not only to state their own position but to deconstruct that of their opponents in order to find the most telling and effective formulation. They try not to weary the other into forgiveness but rather to convince that individual to forgive. They each articulate their beliefs as a critique of the other in an attempt to subvert their opponent's position, to force the opponent to agree and thereby end the argument. The arguments between Congreve's lovers and their women do develop in this way, and it is here, in her critique of the lover, that we find the reasons for the woman's scepticism.

VAINLOVE: For as love is a deity, he must be served by prayer.

BELINDA: O gad, would you all pray to Love then, and let us alone!

VAINLOVE: You are the temples of Love, and 'tis through you our devotion must be conveyed.

ARAMINTA: Rather poor silly idols of your own making, which, upon the least displeasure, you forsake, and set up new.— Every man, now, changes his mistress and his religion as his humour varies or his interest. (TOB, II, ii)

SONG

Thus to a ripe consenting maid,
Poor old, repenting Delia said:—
Would you long preserve your lover?
Would you still his goddess reign?
Never let him all discover,
Never let him much obtain.

Men will admire, adore and die,
While wishing at your feet they lie:
But admitting their embraces
Wakes 'em from their golden dream;
Nothing's new besides our faces,
Every woman is the same. (TOB, II, ii)

VALENTINE: You are not leaving me in this uncertainty?

ANGELICA: Would anything but a madman complain of uncertainty? Uncertainty and expectation are the joys of life. Security is an insipid thing, and the overtaking and possessing of a wish discovers the folly of the chase. Never let us know one another better: for the pleasure of a masquerade is done when we come to show our faces . . . (LL, IV, iii)

For the lover, as we have seen, the reality of his emotions are primary. The ideology of love naturalizes desire, defines it by its immediacy and intensity. The lover "naturally" recognizes the true object of his love and moves toward it in a direct and simple way. In this he is different from the majority of men, who are captured by the apparent necessities of money and convention and are forced by these necessities into the devious pursuit of unnatural ends.

For the women who are the objects of the lover's attention—and who are therefore cast in the role of the natural complement of desire—the perspective is somewhat different. They experience it not as an offer of the natural but as a demand which is not essentially different in kind from the coercive requirements of decorum and convention. A dun for love, remarks Belinda in *The Old Bachelor*, is "the most impertinent and troublesome of duns.—A dun for money will be quiet when he sees his debtor has not the wherewithal; but a dun for love is an eternal torment that never rests" (TOB, II, ii).

For Belinda, then, the fascination of the lover with his beloved is not essentially different from the fascination of a businessman with a debt, except that at some point the businessman can be made to understand that the creditor is bankrupt. Implicit in this analogy is Congreve's association of woman as an image of fulfillment in the economics of love and money as an image of value in the commercial world. Desire, in both cases, is displaced from any "natural" object and binds itself to an image where it can find only visions of satisfaction but never the thing itself. Women, then, are not "temples of Love" (TOB, II, ii), where a godlike power to grant wishes is exercised, but "poor silly idols" of the lover's own making.

"You're a woman," Valentine tells Angelica in *Love for Love*, "one to whom Heaven gave beauty, when it grafted roses on a briar. You are the reflection of Heaven in a pond, and he that leaps at you is sunk. You are all white, a sheet of lovely, spotless paper, when you first are born; but you are to be scrawled and blotted by every goose's quill" (LL, IV, iii). Pretending madness, Valentine unwittingly speaks the truth of the woman's position in Congreve's plays. As something written on, she is defined by her place in the complicated network of wills and written documents which, increasingly, comes to dominate the plots of his plays. In this context she functions in a traditional way as the agency through which property is transferred from one man to another. Her value here is simply the value of the money or property for which she is the token or sign. But this situation suggests how she is also defined by the related but more general circulation of language, which is the gossip or conversation of society. In *The Way of the World*, for example, Fainall blackmails his wife by threatening a public action for divorce which will reveal her previous affair. Unless Lady Wishfort agrees, her daughter will be "consigned by the short-hand writers to the public press; and from thence be transferred to the hands, nay into the throats and lungs, of hawkers, with voices more licentious than the loud flounderman's" (WW, V, ii).

Woman as a reflection of heaven, an icon, on the other hand, seems to define her in the context of the traditional paradigms which govern Renaissance love poetry and which exist, in some sense, in opposition to her economic function. Here her meaning seems to depend on something more primary, more intrinsic, than writing. It rests on her beauty, the "gift" (LL, IV, iii) of heaven. This is a meaning which, seemingly, does not have to be read but can be grasped immediately the moment love is born in the eyes. The openness of the lover's language is simply the expression of the simplicity and immediacy of this instinctive perception. Traditionally this moment would free the lovers from the conditions of the commercial world; for example, the lovers in Donne's "The Good-morrow" can, from the security of their self-enclosed world, scoff at the activity of men of business.

Despite the platonic overtones in Valentine's language, however, the real implications of his comments lie in another direction. The most obvious literary antecedent for Angelica is in Ariosto's *Orlando Furioso*. Here, too, a lover, Orlando, pursues another Angelica to the point of madness. Orlando's madness begins when he wanders into a forest where the trees are hung with verses which address his love. The scene corresponds to many others in Ariosto's epic which dramatize a character's paradoxical experience of both the presence and absence of the object of his or her desire. In most instances this dramatization involves the physical appearance and disappearance of the object. Here, however, it is directly related to Angelica's existence as verse, as sign, and the way the sign can counterfeit presence in the midst of absence. Orlando's madness is caused by the impossibility either of escaping the spell of Angelica's presence or of ever possessing her. Having fallen in love with an image, he finds he cannot transcend the conditions of its existence.[3]

The effect of Valentine's comments, then, is to equate a woman's position in the structures of love with the systems of economics and gossip which govern the conventional world. In neither instance is her meaning intrinsic. She is simply a blank surface which receives a reflection, an inscription. Her meaning has only the reality of this image, a significance which can never answer the need it creates. The obsession of the miser and the obsession of the lover are essentially similar. Both dramatize the fate of a desire which, displaced into the world of signs, can never complete itself.

Valentine equates the madness of the lover with the situation of Narcissus, who, in a similar manner, fails to recognize the nature and source of the image in whose contemplation he literally loses himself. The lover, too, accepts the immediacy of his feeling—the sense of presence evoked by the vision of beauty—accepts it as a revelation of the other's true nature. But, like Narcissus, the lover is captured by a mystifying and imaginary relationship with his own image which he finds in place of the other. It is his beauty he loves, the vision of his own perfection he seeks to join.

Valentine speaks the truth, but he does so unwittingly in his attempt to counterfeit madness. Only moments later he reassumes the language of the sincere lover and proposes to Angelica that they "think of leaving acting, and be ourselves" (LL, IV, iii). Valentine again solicits the honest and open conversation which would mark the natural agreement of lovers. From the perspective of the woman, however, this expresses not a more natural but a more mystified consciousness. For her the exemplars of this language, namely, Prue and Ben, illustrate another truth. They are, after all, stock comedic types. Their characteristics have more to do with literary tradition than with the real world. Their naturalness is a literary artifice, not an expression of authenticity. To hope to speak as Ben and Prue do is to hope—as Lady Wishfort does when she discovers Mr. Fainall's plot to discredit her daughter—that you can "retire to deserts and solitudes, and feed harmless sheep by groves and purling streams . . . and be shepherdesses" (WW, V, ii).

Such an escape is possible only if you can transform yourself into a character in a book. It is no accident, from this point of view, that Valentine's pursuit of Angelica has lead him to the point where, in the opening scenes of *Love for Love*, his life has been reduced to reading and writing. The position of the lover, too, is a literary type whose nature is generated, and inevitably determined, by the status of the sign. His innocence is only the innocence of one who believes naively in the reality of the image.

Such innocence is itself a form of madness. "I am not the fool you take me for," Angelica answers when Valentine urges her to be herself, "and you are mad, and don't know it" (LL, IV, iii). The woman's rejection of the lover is based on her real and articulate understanding of the nature of the lover's desire. She knows that this desire is controlled by his relation to the image which he sees reflected in her place and that his natural and open profession of love are only the expression of his blindness to his real situation.

The woman's scepticism of the lover's offer, then, is based on her awareness that his relation to her is imaginary. The lover accepts the intensity of his love as the sign of its authenticity. The woman, on the other hand, sees that all desire implies a mystified relationship to the image. For Angelica there is no difference between Valentine's love for her, Tattle's obsession with adding to his collection of miniature portraits of women he has possessed, and a miser's fixation on his savings. For her they are all versions of the same uncomfortable situation.

The nature of the woman's scepticism determines, in turn, the development of her argument against the lover. For her the truth of desire can only be seen from the outside. She denies love in order to know and master it. In Congreve's plays the position of the woman is like that of the teacher or theorist who commands a field of study from a point beyond and slightly above it. And, like any good teacher, she intends to educate and demystify her students.

From this point of view, the woman's aggression has a pedagogical intent. The abrupt and maddening ways in which she denies the lover's suit are intended to increase the latter's frustration to the point where he questions his uncritical acceptance of his own feelings. To do this she flaunts her superficiality. She presents herself deliberately as a surface whose only reality is the image which is momentarily reflected there. "Think of you," Mirabell says of Millamant, "think of a whirlwind, though't were in a whirlwind were a case of more steady contemplation; a very tranquillity of mind and mansion" (WW, II, ii). In this way she hopes to make him see that his desire is fixated on an image rather than an object which is its natural complement, and that consequently his frustration is not a moment in love's progress but its enduring truth.

At crucial points the woman is also willing to annotate explicitly her student's situation. The man speaks in the first person with the immediacy of personal experience. When Angelica tells Valentine that "security is an insipid thing" and that "the overtaking and possessing of a wish, discovers the folly of the chase" (LL, IV, iii), she speaks as one who has a knowledge of the nature of desire itself. She speaks in generalities, invoking the authority of a universal truth which can interpret individual experience and demystify its apparent simplicity.

In this way the woman's argument works not only to oppose the man's offer but to convert him, to make him agree with her. In this, really, she seems to have no choice. It is not that Congreve's heroines love their suitors less than they are loved but that they find the terms of the lover's offer totally unacceptable. Since this desire is directed not at the woman herself but at an image of wholeness which is only imaginary and can never be possessed, her acquiescence would only reveal her inadequacy in light of his ideal conception of her. His desire would always reappear in another fantasized relationship beyond their particular situation.

In a curious way, then, Congreve's heroines can only express their love effectively through denial. In refusing, she will never be possessed and, never being possessed, she will never be abandoned. At the very least the lover will remain eternally at a fixed distance from her and, consequently, will remain eternally fascinated. This is the wisdom of Araminta's song from *The Old Bachelor*, "Would you long preserve your lover? . . . / Never let him all discover, / Never let him much obtain" (TOB, II, ii).

At best, however, the lover would understand his situation and see the necessity for this distance himself. If Angelica could convince Valentine that it would be "folly" to come to "know one another better" (LL, IV, iii), he would be content with their separation. Both, then, would speak the detached language of the theorist, a language which can express the truth of desire in a way that frees them from its bondage. Their conversation would be the conversation of Merteuil and Valmont in *Les Liaisons dangereuses*—cool, ironic, distanced. They, too, could put the illusions of love behind them and find one another instead in their mutual understanding of its impossibility. It is this conversation which Angelica seems to be offering Valentine when she warns that "the pleasure of a masquerade is done when we come to show our faces" (LL, IV, iii).

In these plays there is at least one man who accepts the woman's offer. If Araminta in *The Old Bachelor* is a "kind of floating-island" who "sometimes seems in reach, then vanishes, and keeps [Vainlove] busied in the search" (TOB, I, i), her evasiveness is easily matched by Vainlove's own. Vainlove avoids any situation, however trivial, which might suggest the possibility of satisfaction. When he seduces a woman, he delivers to his friend Bellmour the task of consummating the adventure. "He does the drudgery in the mine, and you stamp your image on the gold" (TOB, I, i), Heartwell remarks to Bellmour.

Although Vainlove will admit to Bellmour that he loves Araminta, he "plays the fool with discretion" (TOB, I, i), a discretion which equals hers. But this suppression of their active love for one another does not even lead them to the complicated and interesting conversation which occurs between Merteuil and Valmont in a similar situation. Instead, they remain fixed at a given distance from one another. At the end of the play, when Bellmour and Belinda marry, Vainlove and Araminta can only agree to an indefinite postponement of their own wedding. In refusing to play the fool, they do not escape love's frustrations but are condemned to live them in passive silence. In this *The Old Bachelor* seems to imply a certain scepticism vis-à-vis the "truth" of the woman's detachment, which, from this position, becomes a kind of solitary confinement. Certainly this is borne out by the lovers in Congreve's later plays. They are not so easily seduced by the detachment and control of women and are more willing than Vainlove to insist on their own feelings.

IF MORE OF CONGREVE'S LOVERS are not convinced by the woman's vision, it is undoubtedly because they do not experience it as the statement of an abstract and objective truth. When the woman confronts the fixity of the lover's desire with her own unpredictability and variety, he does not see it as the enactment of a liberating knowledge but rather as the expression of a harsh and arbitrary authority. However well-meaning her performance, the lover inevitably feels not only that it is given at his expense but that for this very reason its pretensions to truth are hypocritical. It is, after all, his generosity which has provided the context for her display and his constancy which keeps him there as its audience. It is not truth which has conferred freedom but rather his own forbearance. The woman has conveniently suppressed his role in this, but the man is not fooled. In the words of Mellefont's song from *The Double-Dealer*, "Cynthia frowns whene'er I woo her, / Yet she's vexed if I give over; / Much she fears I should undo her, / But much more to lose her lover" (DD, II, i).

In its most sophisticated form, the man's response to the woman's scepticism is not a simple renewal of his initial offer or an abject acceptance of the woman's argument. Instead he directs his attention to the woman's assumption that she somehow transcends desire. Initially the lover had claimed to speak a language which was the direct and natural expression of love and, therefore, beyond the misrepresentations of conventional discourse. The woman has shown that this language is in fact generated by an image, and that its simplicity is itself a figure of speech, a lie. But from the man's point of view the woman seems to make a similar assumption. She, too, claims to speak the language of truth, to describe the situation of love in a way that frees her from its misrepresentations. To him this seems more than questionable.

Mirabell, in a scene with Millamant from *The Way of the World*, addresses this issue directly and it is worth quoting their exchange at some length. Their argument begins over an incident the previous evening in which Mirabell had been banished so that Millamant and her aunt could gossip with two fops, Petulant and Witwoud.

MILLAMANT: Mirabell, did you take exception last night? Oh ay, and went away.—Now I think on't I'm angry—no, now I think on't I'm pleased—for I believe I gave you some pain.

MIRABELL: Does that please you?

MILLAMANT: Infinitely; I love to give pain.

MIRABELL: You would affect a cruelty which is not in your nature; your true vanity is in the power of pleasing.

MILLAMANT: Oh I ask your pardon for that—one's cruelty is one's power; and when one parts with one's cruelty, one parts with one's power; and when one has parted with that, I fancy one's old and ugly.

MIRABELL: Ay, ay, suffer your cruelty to ruin the object of your power, to destroy your lover—and then how vain, how lost a thing you'll be! Nay, 'tis true: you are no longer handsome when you've lost your lover; your beauty dies upon the instant; for beauty is the lover's gift; 'tis he bestows your charms—your glass is all a cheat. The ugly and the old, whom the looking-glass mortifies, yet after commendation can be flattered by it, and discovers beauties in it; for that reflects our praises, rather than your face.

MILLAMANT: O the vanity of these men!—Fainall, d'ye hear him? If they did not commend us, we were not handsome! Now you must know that they could not commend one, if one was not handsome. Beauty the lover's gift! Lord, what is a lover, that it can give? Why one makes lovers as fast as one pleases, and they live as long as one pleases, and they die as soon as one pleases; and then, if one pleases, one makes more.
. . . . . . . . . . . . . . . . . . . . . . . . . . . . . . . . . . . . . . . . . . . . . . . . . . . .
One no more owes one's beauty to a lover, than one's wit to an echo. They can but reflect what we look and say; vain empty things if we are silent or unseen, and want a being.

MIRABELL: Yet to those two vain empty things you owe the two greatest pleasures of your life.

MILLAMANT: How so?

MIRABELL: To your lover you owe the pleasure of hearing yourself praised; and to an echo the pleasure of hearing yourself talk. (WW, II, ii)

In this scene Millamant enacts once again the heroine's refusal of the lover. But she enacts it in a particularly interesting manner. We might think for a moment about the way this scene allows us to understand how the respective assumptions of the lover and the woman inform their actual experience. In this confrontation Millamant speaks not the truth of her position but its power. She does not find the meaning of her role in the detached objectivity of its vision but rather in the joy of refusal which this objectivity confers.

Another way to understand Millamant's attitude would be to see it as the result of a process of recuperation. Millamant, we know, loves Mirabell "violently" (WW, IV, i). But on the previous night she has rejected him, preferring the superficial distraction of Witwoud and Petulant to the seriousness of love. In doing this she sacrifices her own true feeling, her own love for Mirabell. In her initial refusal to answer the lover in his own language, the woman, as we have seen, has no choice. The lover's desire is for something which transcends her, something for which she is only the image. Her superficiality is simply a way of asserting her understanding of this situation.

The necessity of this initial refusal, however, does nothing to change the fact that it is a sacrifice. It cuts Millamant off from the instinctive and natural level of experience, which makes us feel most at home and comfortable in the world. This is precisely the level of experience which the lover flaunts before her in such a naive and lavish way. He constantly tempts her to accept his image of her and, in doing so, to express her desire for him naturally.

It would be wrong to think that Millamant is not tempted. As we have seen, Congreve's heroines, like their lovers, refuse to live according to the conventional terms of their world. Their lovers seem to offer them a positive life outside of these terms, one which is not simply a cold withdrawal. Such a withdrawal has little real appeal for these women. All of them, like Araminta, could call for "oil to feed that flame" (TOB, II, ii). They are not cold women but rather women who do not believe in the possibility of their desire. In *The Double-Dealer* Cynthia, depressed by the spectacle of Lord and Lady Froth's foolish marriage, finds herself discouraged at the prospect of her own marriage to Mellefont. " 'Tis an odd game we're going to play at," she says, adding, "what think you of drawing stakes, and giving over in time?" "No, hang't," he replies, "that's not endeavouring to win, because it's possible we may lose" (DD, II, i). Congreve's women are always ready to cut their losses not because they do not care but because, from their point of view, loss seems inevitable.

It is little wonder that a Millamant or an Angelica would direct a certain exasperated hostility toward a lover who staged for them a version of their own instinctive feelings of love while simultaneously illustrating so clearly the mystified nature of these feelings. But Millamant's comments allow us to see that her cruelty is not simply the expression of her resentment at her sacrifice. It is a way of recovering this sacrifice, of receiving something else in exchange.

This is clear in Millamant's identification of cruelty, power, and beauty: ". . . when one parts with one's cruelty, one parts with one's power; and when one has parted with that, I fancy one's old and ugly." The lover had made her beauty an image—his image—and in doing so he has alienated her from it, forced her to deny it. This denial is justified, rationalized, by her understanding of the imaginary nature of the lover's desire. This understanding, in turn, allows her to be free of his desire, to reject it, in a way that returns her beauty to her in the joy of refusal, as the exercise of power. She contemplates herself in the unhappy face of the rejected lover and recovers herself in the infinite pleasure of cruelty.

Lovers, for Millamant, are only mirrors who "can but reflect what we look and say" (WW, II, ii). But as soon as she says this, it is easy to see that, in this act of recuperation, the woman's position has simply become another version of the lover's. Like the lover, Millamant now finds herself in an image located in another and acts to assume this image. The fact that she can inflict pain on Mirabell does nothing to change her basic dependence on him. This is the force of Mirabell's argument, which emphasizes the inevitable dependence of the master on the slave.

Mirabell's reply shows us that as soon as Millamant speaks her position, as soon as she formulates her transcendence of desire as a refusal, it becomes enmeshed again in the imaginary relation between the woman and the lover. In her refusal, then, she does not escape desire but merely displaces it. Millamant is ensnared by the fascinating image of herself which she contemplates in the unhappy face of her lover. She sees happiness in the attempt to live her name, to create a thousand lovers who reflect this power. But in this she is not different from Tattle and his collection of miniatures. She, too, stands in an equally mystified relation to the image, attempting to find satisfaction in the accumulation of representations.

AT THIS POINT WE CAN SEE that the argument between the lover and the woman has reached something of a standoff. Both had begun by asserting the authenticity of their position. Each had claimed to stand apart from the corrupt desires of the conventional world. But in their exchange each shows the other's pretensions to be exactly that. The lover believes his offer is the natural expression of feeling; the woman believes that her detachment is free and objective. Both attitudes now appear as simple fascinations with an image which are not essentially different from more conventional manifestations of the same kind of fixation.

It is amusing to think for a moment about the symmetry which we can now see exists between the romantic and married couples in these plays. Both manifest the effects of the inevitable disjunction between an image of fulfillment and an inadequate reality. In the face of this disjunction there are only two alternatives, and these alternatives describe the limited possibilities of both love and marriage. It is possible to engage in a ceaseless pursuit of an (endless) series of images, constantly moving from expectation through possession and disappointment to renewed fascination. This possibility can be experienced by the man as a rake, a philandering husband, or, in the sense that this is also the rhythm of greed, as an acquisitive suitor. It can be experienced by the woman who is sexually aggressive or by the unresponsive beauty who possesses an innumerable hoard of suitors.

On the other hand, it is possible to live at a fixed distance from one image. This alternative can be experienced by the woman in the obsession of Lady Touchwood for Mellefont or of Mrs. Marwood for Mirabell. It can be experienced by the man as the devoted lover or as a certain kind of dissatisfied and encumbered husband. In the latter case the frustration which the lover experiences in a projective form as longing is experienced by the husband as a claustrophobic imprisonment.

Given these limited possibilities, it is clear that any agreement

between the lover and the woman which would result either winning the argument on his or her own terms could take only a
very uncomfortable and superficial form. Since both the man's
generosity and the woman's refusal are an attempt, really, to
unite with their own image, the idea of an agreement which is the
product of one party winning the argument inevitably implies
their coincidence with this image. Each hopes to find in the other's acquiescence an impossible agreement with themselves. But
this moment can only bring disillusionment; the woman will inevitably seek new subjects, and the lover a new fascination.

Congreve's most concise example of this situation is provided
by the characters of Lord and Lady Froth in *The Double-Dealer*.
Early in the second act the two re-create for Cynthia the moment in their courtship when Lady Froth gave Lord Froth her
miniature portrait. In a scene that needs little commentary, she
gives him her pocket mirror instead. "Nay, my lord," she says
finally, "you shan't kiss it so much, I shall grow jealous" (DD,
II, i).

Froth, of course, won this argument, succeeded in the suit,
and apparently lives with his wife in a fulsome and demonstrative
wedded bliss. "My lord," says Lady Froth, "I have been telling
Cynthia how much I have been in love with you, I swear I have;
I'm not ashamed to own it now" (DD, II, i). But despite the fact
that Lord Froth has received that explicit response which the
lover desires, it has hardly brought him happiness, much less bliss.
Lord Froth, we learn, actually possesses his wife only rarely.
"Did not she tell you at what a distance she keeps him?" Mellefont asks Careless. "He has confessed to me that but at some certain times . . . he never has the privilege of using the familiarity
of a husband with a wife. He was once given to scrambling with
his hands and sprawling in his sleep; and ever since she has him
swaddled up in blankets . . . and there he lies with a great beard,
like a Russian bear upon a drift of snow" (DD, III, ii).

Lord Froth has found beyond the acceptance of the woman
only a particularly unpleasant version of the dissatisfaction of the
lover. But the same is true of Lady Froth. "Ah, that look," Lord
Froth says to his wife, "t'was so my heart was made captive first,
and ever since 't has been in love with happy slavery" (DD, II,

i). But although he accepts his role as slave, as the reflection of his wife's power, it does not satisfy her. The only time she does give herself to her husband, we learn, is when she is pregnant from one of her many affairs.

Lord and Lady Froth are, of course, fools. Congreve's lovers and their women seem more intelligent, less blind to their own ridiculousness. Certainly couples such as these could recognize their situation, come to some understanding, and acknowledge their feelings for each other in a rational way. Once they have been shown the error of their position by their respective partners, then surely they can detach themselves from the exaggerated roles of pleading lover and reluctant woman and laugh together at their own foolishness. In this laughter they could find another, better way to agree.

It is clear that this question lies behind Congreve's interest in the argument between the lover and the woman. He is especially concerned with the period between the birth of love—a moment which is never dramatized or given any real emphasis in his work—and its formalization. His subject, really, is this period of negotiation during which couples attempt to decide the terms of their marriage. From this point of view, the conflict in these plays is not the product of an opposition between convention and love, since the relationship between the man and the woman in both cases is determined by desire's fixation on an image of its own completion. The real tension is between the way desire seems to determine our relation to the other—making that individual either the sign of a hoped-for completion or a present inadequacy—and the sense we have that, because we are able to talk about this situation, we can structure and control it.

In this context the Froths' marriage is a more disturbing example. The Froths are fools *now*, of course. But if we look more closely we can see that in their marriage each has, in fact, tried to take the other into consideration. Each has affirmed the other's desire, become the consenting woman and the happily enslaved lover. It is this agreement that is honored in their rhetorical proclamations of love. But what has determined their situation is not this intention but rather the logic of a desire which, in spite of this agreement, still binds them not to the other but to an image.

Their agreement has simply blinded them to this fact. It is what makes them foolish instead of only disillusioned or realistic in the manner of, say, Fainall and his wife in *The Way of the World*.

The Froths' foolishness, then, is not occasional but a sign of the failure of a certain conversation. This is the rational conversation of a man and a woman who have reached the same impasse as other lovers in these plays and have said to each other, in contemporary terms, "Look, this is stupid. We know we both care for each other. Let's talk about it"—the conversation, in other words, which self-consciously begins again in an attempt to master and redefine its situation.

Again, how can such openness and honesty lead to such foolishness? With this question in mind, we might consider in greater detail the scene between Valentine and Angelica in *Love for Love*, where each seems, in fact, to attempt to begin again and to offer one another a different kind of response.

> VALENTINE: You see what disguises love makes us put on: gods have been in counterfeited shapes for the same reason; and the divine part of me, my mind, has worn this mask of madness, and this motley livery, only as the slave of love, and menial creature of your beauty.
>
> ANGELICA: Mercy on me, how he talks! poor Valentine!
>
> VALENTINE: Nay, faith, now let us understand one another, hypocrisy apart.—The comedy draws toward an end, and let us think of leaving acting, and be ourselves; and since you have loved me, you must own, I have at length deserved you should confess it.
>
> ANGELICA: (*Sighs*) I would I have loved you!—For Heaven knows I pity you; and could I have foreseen the bad effects, I would have striven; but that's too late.
>
> VALENTINE: What bad effects?—what's too late? My seeming madness has deceived my father, and procured me time to think of means to reconcile me to him, and preserve the right of my inheritance to his estate; which otherwise by articles I must this morning have resigned . . .
>
> ANGELICA: How! I thought your love of me had caused this transport in your soul; which, it seems, you only counterfeited for mercenary ends and sordid interest.
>
> . . . . . . . . . . . . . . . . . . . . . . . . . . . . . . . . . . . . . . . . . . . . . . . . . . . . . . .
>
> VALENTINE: Oh, 'tis barbarous to misunderstand me longer.
>
> . . . . . . . . . . . . . . . . . . . . . . . . . . . . . . . . . . . . . . . . . . . . . . . . . . . . . . .

VALENTINE: You are not leaving me in this uncertainty?

ANGELICA: Would anything but a madman complain of uncertainty? Uncertainty and expectation are the joys of life. Security is an insipid thing, and the overtaking and possessing of a wish discovers the folly of the chase. Never let us know one another better: for the pleasure of a masquerade is done, when we come to show our faces; but I'll tell you two things before I leave you; I am not the fool you take me for; and you are mad, and don't know it.

VALENTINE: From a riddle you can expect nothing but a riddle . . . She is a medal without a reverse or inscription, for indifference has both sides alike. (LL, IV, iii)

The situation in this case is somewhat more complicated by the immediate dramatic context. *Love for Love* is a play about exchange and, specifically, about Angelica's refusal to exchange love for money. To win her Valentine must prove his love by divesting it of any possible economic motive. (It is a play, in other words, about both the necessity and the difficulty of communicating an intention clearly.) At this point Valentine has bankrupted himself and is being forced by his creditors to sell the rights to his inheritance. To prevent this he counterfeits madness.

For Angelica, then, there is, at least ostensibly, a question about Valentine's motives. But this does not change the basic issue. Here the lover tries to step out of his "motley"—and confining—disguise and discuss his condition rationally. For Angelica to accept Valentine's offer it would not be necessary for her to accept him completely. We could imagine a conversation emerging from this situation in which she voiced her doubts about his intentions and he justified himself; of course he has attempted to save his inheritance. They will need something to live on, and so forth. It would be enough that she acknowledged his attempt to discuss things reasonably. There would then be a conversation between them outside of, and above, their initial exchange of offer and refusal. This would be the metaconversation of the lover and the woman in which their initial gestures would be discussed, analyzed, and justified.

Angelica, however, refuses absolutely. In doing so she returns the lover to his original position. Valentine's offer to discuss his love is treated as his original offer itself, subject to the same suspicions and scepticism. This moment becomes simply the repetition of all the other encounters between the two.

The fact of this repetition, however, does allow us to see the mechanism which is operating here, the mechanism which subverts Valentine's heroic attempts to express himself clearly. Valentine's intention is to step out of his role as lover, to make his offer on another level, in another way. But Angelica does not respond to this change in intention. She reacts to what is continuous and persistent in their situation, the constant pressure of Valentine's offering. In this she is not entirely mistaken. This persistence does have a significance all its own. Valentine is a man who has spent a considerable amount of time being in love with a woman who has never responded to him. As Scandal remarks, Valentine's decision to disinherit himself is "a very desperate demonstration of your love to Angelica; and I think she has never given you any assurance of hers" (LL, I, ii). The apparent sense of Valentine's language to Angelica has always been that of openness, generosity, and sacrifice. It is only when this language is placed in the context of her refusal and silence, and meets it head on, that another meaning emerges from the discontinuity between offer and response. The persistence of the lover's offer in any form reveals its obsessive quality and inclines us to see it as simply another manifestation of the lover's absolute demand. An offer, after all, is made with the assumption that it may be freely refused. To offer something relentlessly is to imply something else entirely. It is this implication, the demand that is the meaning of his love, which Valentine cannot escape and which is revealed to him when his intentions are returned to him inverted in Angelica's refusal.

This is the truth, then, of Angelica's misunderstanding, which associates Valentine's offer with the obsession of greed. But, obviously, a similar situation exists at the end of this scene. Angelica here seems to annotate her silence, to open up the space for a conversation about her detachment, when she asks, "Would anything but a madman complain of uncertainty?" (LL, IV, iii) When her intention meets Valentine's frustration, however, it undergoes a similar inversion. If we suspend, for a moment, our awareness of the happy ending of *Love for Love* and focus instead on Angelica's enjoyment of Valentine's misery, we can see that in these moments she is a sister to Millamant. Valentine's frustration returns even the most rational and detached refusal to her as the seductive vision of her own power.

Valentine intends to state his love rationally and signifies his demand. Angelica intends to voice her refusal rationally and signifies her desire for power. In each case the apparent offer of a rational conversation only intensifies the other's obsession: Valentine's generosity only reinforces Angelica's sense of power; Angelica's detachment only intensifies Valentine's generosity. And so it goes in a process which, it seems, has several possible endings but no apparent resolution.

This is one way to understand what Cynthia means when she remarks that she has seen "two wits meet, and by the opposition of their wit render themselves as ridiculous as fools" (DD, II, i). Her comment is inspired, after all, by the example of the Froths' marriage. And we can now see that this marriage has been structured by the same dialectic in which an attempt at rational agreement has been subverted by the persistent and defining action of desire.

These examples suggest why the couples in these plays are unable to reach an agreement based on a sane understanding of their situation, are unable, in other words, to have a conversation which acknowledges desire directly and, in doing so, allows them to control it. These characters are nothing if not verbal. But, from a certain point of view, it is their sense of their own verbal facility which is their undoing. Both the lovers and their women identify with their language, feel committed to it as the expression of their intention. In both cases, however, the effective meaning of their statements is not determined by this intention but by the statement's effect on the listener. And in both cases the inversion of the speaker's intention which occurs at the moment of reception reveals that this meaning is interpreted by the other as an expression of the law of desire, of its absolute demand for an impossible fulfillment.

The speaker's ideal of a perfectly direct and comprehensible expression of his intention is only a version of the lover's ideal of perfect, unmediated love or the woman's vision of infinite power. Like the lover, the speaker who intends his conversation to be the clear and full expression of his meaning listens, in the place of the other, only for his own echo, understands only himself. In both cases the real significance of these messages is a function of desire's fascination with this image and its absolute demand to coincide with it. Like the lover, the more the speaker insists on his meaning and clarifies himself, the more it is apparent to everyone but himself that the true significance of his language lies not in its superficial expression of an intentionality but in the intensity of his desire for an understanding which would mark this coincidence.

It is not hard to understand this situation. Undoubtedly we have all been stopped—usually on the way to some important appointment—by a colleague who spends an unconscionably long time making himself clear on some issue. The more he concerns himself with our understanding of his message, the less we feel taken into account. He ignores our increasingly frantic signals in the same way Valentine ignores Angelica's coldness. We simply become mirrors which reflect a power as narcissistic as that which Millamant exercises over Mirabell.

What is worse, we have undoubtedly found ourselves imprisoning our colleagues in this way, ignoring their efforts to disengage themselves, watching their increasing discomfort and anger with a strange bewilderment at our own failure to stop. At moments such as these we can understand most clearly the persistence of Congreve's lovers and the real meaning of this persistence—which has nothing to do with communication in an intersubjective sense and everything to do with making ourselves understood as a way of forcing a perfectly articulated image of ourselves on our correspondent.

In such situations, too, we can understand what is involved in the impossibility of finding some metalanguage which transcends desire and allows couples to address one another outside of its determining effects. Since such a language is impossible in Congreve's world, to speak is inevitably to be caught up in a desire for the articulated image of yourself which your language works to locate in the place of your listeners by persuading them, making them understand you. The more directly one speaks—the more one's language aims, like the lover's, at some ideal of natural expressiveness, or, like the woman's, at some ideal of detached clarity—the more this will be true. Regardless of the explicit content of the message, the speaker's desire to have it completely understood always bears on his desire to find his articulated image in his listener. In this sense both speakers talk only to this image—to themselves, in effect—and their message is always the same. It is always a statement of that impossible demand. It would be difficult, for example, to think of two conversational styles which are more different than Valentine's and Angelica's. But, as we have seen, both finally signify this desire, and the intensity of this signification is a function of a persistent commitment to their intentions—the lover to his generosity and the woman to the "truth" which justifies her refusal.

Clearly, any reconciliation between the lover and the woman cannot be the result of some simple exchange in which each would express his or her desire in a direct way and the other would understand and accept it. This kind of mutual understanding could only produce some version of the Froths' marriage, which, again, is based on a similar exchange. It follows, by a strange logic, that the only agreement which would avoid the trap of the Froths' relationship would be one which maintained difference and opposition. In this context, to accept difference is to accept the inevitability of being misunderstood. Both the lover and the woman resign themselves to the fact that their message would return from the other in a fragmented and distorted form. They would exist for each other not as the possible location of an imagined unity but as that which frustrates this unity. But in this frustration each would locate the existence of the other as otherness, difference, and this would, in turn, allow for the possibility of a conversation which, to some extent, escapes the fundamental narcissism behind the desire for understanding.

It is interesting to consider, in this connection, the most well-known agreement between Congreve's lovers, namely, the contract scene between Millamant and Mirabell in *The Way of the World*. In this scene the two negotiate the terms of their married life. Mirabell accepts certain limitations on his prerogatives as a husband. Millamant will have the "liberty to pay and receive visits to and from whom I please; to write and receive letters, without interrogatories or wry faces on your part; to . . . come to dinner when I please; dine in my dressing room when I'm out of humor, without giving a reason. To have my closet inviolate;

to be sole Empress of my tea table, which you must never approach without first asking leave" (WW, IV, i). In return, she will surrender to Mirabell the affectations of fashionable existence. She will admit no female confidante as a "decoy duck, to wheedle you a fop-scrambling the play in a mask." She will abandon all painting and "endeavor not to new-coin" her face (WW, IV, i).

At the end of their exchange, Mirabell exclaims, "Then we are agreed! shall I kiss your hand upon the contract?" (WW, IV, i) It would be tempting to read this contract as a version of the understanding between Pamela and B, an agreement between lovers that frees them from their differences and validates, in an unambiguous way, the sense we have that they are special and escape the conditions of their world. But if we consider this moment in the context of the exchange which immediately precedes it, we can see that it is much more reasonable to view their contract as a kind of restaging or reformulation of their opposition rather than a transcendence of it. The scene begins when Mirabell enters and warns Millamant that she "can fly no further." Consider, from this point of view, the first exchange of this scene. "No," she replies, "I'll fly and be followed to the last moment . . . I'll be solicited to the very last, nay, and afterwards" (WW, IV, i). Her position in marriage will be a certain version of her stance during courtship. While she may perhaps "by degrees dwindle into a wife," it will never reach the point where Mirabell could display "the saucy look of an assured man, confident of success" (WW, IV, i).

Unlike Angelica, Millamant's coldness is not simply a "dissembling" which will turn to "extreme fondness" (LL, V, ii) after marriage. "Oh, I should think I was poor and had nothing to bestow, if I were reduced to an inglorious ease, and freed from the agreeable fatigues of solicitation" (WW, IV, i), she says. Despite her sacrifices Millamant is still defined primarily by her power and by the resistance which it offers to the lover's demand. But in accepting Mirabell she accepts certain limits on this power and, consequently, a certain discrepancy between them, a certain disjunction between her vision of the omnipotent beauty and the fact of Mirabell's rights as a husband. She accepts, in other words, that he will not always agree with her.

But the same can be said for Mirabell who, in undertaking this task of endless solicitation, recognizes certain limits on his prerogatives. He will never discover himself in the natural correspondence which the lover dreams he will find with the woman, but will continue to be separated from her by her assertion of power, by the necessity to knock and solicit entry. Mirabell's provisos do not attempt to modify Millamant's limitations on their intimacy. Instead, they restrict the way she will circulate in society. Mirabell demands that Millamant will "admit no friend to screen her affairs under countenance" (WW, IV, i). He demands, in other words, that she will not become another Lady Froth and compensate for his limitations on her power by creating a thousand other lovers. Just as he must accept the frustration of a less-than-total intimacy, she must accept the frustration of a less-than-total power.

This is another conception of the contract not as the agency of agreement but as a formulation of the differences between fundamentally irreconcilable parties. In this sense it does resolve the opposition between Millamant and Mirabell, but it does so by making the fact of their difference explicit. The argument between the lover and the woman is the argument between two absolute demands, the relentless generosity of the lover and the implacable selfishness of the woman. Resolution here can only mean a certain acceptance of frustration.

For Millamant and Mirabell this is not an acceptance which takes the form of a philosophic wisdom which pretends to rise above desire itself. This form of "wisdom," again, leads most often not to transcendence but to the acceptance of the most stereotyped forms of cynicism. Millamant and Mirabell are not arranging a life in which they contemplate one another quietly from a safe distance, like two enemies who have exhausted one another and finally decided that passivity is the better part of valor. The energy with which they negotiate with one another makes it clear that they will continue to resist and pursue.

They do not abandon desire but live a desire which has, to some extent, been liberated from its obsessive fixation on an image of its own fulfillment. But this allows it to become desire for another. It allows each to feel the other's presence, to converse with one another. This conversation will, of course, be an argument, but one which takes place on different terms. Acceptance of frustration demystifies the idea of winning, with its implication of completion. What remains is argument as the unresolvable play of difference in which the opponents find one another in their resistance to one another, in the collision of argument and rebuttal. The positions of the lover and the woman are divested of their pretensions to truth and become simply a rhetorical opposition which generates their difference. It is no longer the conclusion of the argument which fascinates but the process of arguing itself, since it is in this argument that they have, finally, found one another.

This might seem like a somewhat ingenuous interpretation of what, on the surface, is the most ordinary kind of domestic understanding. But Congreve himself provides the best gloss on Millamant and Mirabell's contract in a conversation between Cynthia and Mellefont in *The Double-Dealer*. This encounter—which occurs in the opening scene of the fourth act, at a moment when their engagement is most threatened by Lady Touchwood—involves a comparable bit of negotiation with similar results.

CYNTHIA: I'll lay my life it will never come to be a match.
MELLEFONT: What?
CYNTHIA: Between you and me.
MELLEFONT: Why so?
CYNTHIA: My mind gives me it won't—because we are both willing; we each of us strive to reach the goal, and hinder one another in the race; I swear it never does well when the parties are so agreed.—For when people walk hand in hand, there's neither overtaking nor meeting: we hunt in couples, where we both pursue the same game, but forget one another; and tis because we are so near that we don't think of coming together.
MELLEFONT: Hum, 'gad, I believe there's something in't;—marriage is the game that we hunt, and while we think that we only have it in view, I don't see but we have it in our power.
CYNTHIA: Within reach; for example, give me your hand; you have looked through the wrong end of the perspective all this while; for nothing has been between us but our fears.
MELLEFONT: I don't know why we should not steal out of the house this very moment, and marry one another, without

consideration, or the fear of repentance. Pox'o fortune, portion, settlements, and jointures!

CYNTHIA: Ay, ay, what have we to do with 'em?—you know we
marry for love.

MELLEFONT: Love, love, downright, very villainous love.

CYNTHIA: And he that can't live upon love deserves to die in a
ditch. Here, then, I give you my promise, in spite of duty,
any temptation of wealth, your inconstancy, or my own inclination to change—

MELLEFONT: To run most willfully and unreasonably away with
me at this moment, and be married.

CYNTHIA: Hold!—never to marry anybody else.

MELLEFONT: That's but a negative consent.—Why, you won't balk
the frolic?

CYNTHIA: If you had not been so assured of your own conduct I
would not;—but 'tis very reasonable that since I consent to
like a man without the vile consideration of money, he would
give me a very evident demonstration of his wit: therefore let
me see you undermine my Lady Touchwood, as you boasted,
and force her to give her consent, and then—

MELLEFONT: I'll do't.

CYNTHIA: And I'll do't. (DD, IV, i)

Up to this point in the play Cynthia and Mellefont have been
joined in a concerted attempt to protect their engagement against
the efforts of the jealous Lady Touchwood to discredit him. At
first glance it seems that Cynthia is saying something very simple
and obvious, namely, that in their concern with the political ma-
neuverings surrounding these plots she and Mellefont have lost
their awareness of each other. Their cooperation in frustrating
these schemes, in pursuing a conventional marriage which would
assure their inheritance, has blinded them to the real possibilities
of their love. When Cynthia gives Mellefont her hand, it is to affirm these possibilities. Their concern with complex legal manipulations, although it has seemed a cooperative enterprise, has really
been a forgetting of one another. The joining of their hands
seems to declare the reality of a love which can ignore "portions,
settlements and jointures" (DD, IV, i).

But the simplicity of this apparently romantic meaning is immediately compromised when Cynthia demands Mellefont's vic-

tory over Lady Touchwood as a precondition of her consent to marry. Cynthia declares the freedom of love to unite them only to reject this possibility. Instead, the lovers turn back to the very situation which has separated them—financial necessity, the jealousy of Lady Touchwood—and appropriate it, make it the context of a wager between them. Rather than marrying for love they choose to stand opposed to one another as players on opposite sides in a game. Their joining of hands, then, has much the same effect as the similar gesture which seals the negotiations between Mirabell and Millamant. Both mark a certain formalization of the relationship between lovers which recognizes and incorporates their difference and opposition.

This wager between Mellefont and Cynthia is, really, an extension of an earlier conversation between them. "Marriage," Mellefont remarks, "is rather like a game at bowls; Fortune indeed makes the match, and the two nearest, and sometimes the two farthest, are together; but the game depends entirely upon judgement." "Still it is a game," Cynthia replies, "and consequently one of us must be a loser." "Not at all," Mellefont answers, "only a friendly trial of skill, and the winnings to be laid out in an entertainment" (DD, II, i). By putting the possibility of their marriage into play, Cynthia forces Mellefont to realize his words and accept himself, his trivialization of winning. The force of the bet which she imposes on them is directed against the assurance of his own conduct which Cynthia's acknowledgment of her love has instilled in him. Mellefont, in other words, is acting as if he has, in fact, won his argument with her in some final way. In response to this, she formulates a game which will demand that both again wager the grounds of their assurance. For Mellefont this is Cynthia's total consent and the imagination of fulfillment which it implies. For Cynthia it is the power to refuse and to find herself in the effect of this refusal. Their marriage, she implies, will be possible only on condition that it is a continuous, if friendly, test of skill in which winning is a moment which is immediately "laid out in an entertainment" (DD, IV, i). Winning, in other words, is never the final point of the game, the moment which will determine the fixed structure of their relationship. Winning is subordinated to the process of the game itself, so that

the moment of triumph occurs only to be risked again and returned to play.

What emerges from this agreement to oppose one another is a
certain conversation between the lover and the woman which is
neither the explicit exchange of the Froths nor the absolute refusal to express their feelings which characterizes Vainlove and
Araminta at the end of *The Old Bachelor*. Here Cynthia does admit her love. But as soon as she says it openly, she immediately
modifies her statement. She does not deny it, but she retracts what
is positive in it. Finally she gives Mellefont only a negative consent. She promises not to marry any of her other suitors. From
this Mellefont might infer that she loves him. But he does not
hear it explicitly and, consequently, cannot rest assured in his
feelings.

Cynthia moves the conversation from a level on which love can
only be explicitly stated or denied—a situation which defines the
initial argument between Congreve's lovers—to one where the expression of love exists on a level of connotation or implication.
Moreover, she insists that Mellefont do likewise. Under the terms
of the wager, Mellefont must displace his love and express it
through his successful opposition to Lady Touchwood's maneu-
vers. He, too, must offer his love indirectly, by implication. In
her reformulation of their argument, then, the basic opposition
between the two is preserved. The man still offers; the woman
still refuses. But, to some extent, their conversation escapes the
lure of explicit statement and complete understanding. The assured lover speaks openly and directly and assumes that he will be
responded to in the same way. The lover who wagers, who denies
the illusions of assurance, must, like Mellefont, depend on his wit
and be content with the implicit.

Implication in this sense is that which is opposed to the clarity
of explicit meaning. Cynthia's statement that she will marry no
other means just that. What it implies is more difficult to state
precisely because connotations never manifest themselves in a
clear and distinct way. In an exchange which proceeds in this
way, neither participant will ever find his or her intention clearly
reflected in the other's response. An argument which accepts this
condition is an argument in which the opponents understand that

it will never be resolved by one party's explicit acceptance of the other's truth. To put desire into play, then, is to accept both the inevitability and necessity of deferral. A game which is played "as a friendly trial of skill" (DD, IV, i), with the understanding that the winnings will be spent generously, is a game which stresses the activity of playing, not the result. Here play is nothing but the artful elaboration of opposing positions. Cynthia and Mellefont will not live together in the peace of perfect understanding. Their marriage will be a witty and interminable argument over trivial matters.

Cynthia's comments about lovers who "strive to reach the goal, and hinder one another in the race" (DD, IV, i) apply not only to couples who might lose sight of one another in the pursuit of some practical objective but to any attempt by lovers to agree with one another. She and Mellefont join hands to mark the possibility of union for "villainous love" (DD, IV, i) but separate immediately, since "it never goes well when the parties are so agreed" (DD, IV, i). The understanding which the lover and the woman initially seek is always bought at the expense of the other, who is lost in this correspondence and is transformed into an image of the self. Since the other can be recognized and addressed only as that which resists correspondence, for Mellefont and Cynthia to continue to love each other they must continue to wager, to play against one another, and find one another in this argument, for "when people walk hand in hand, there's neither overtaking nor meeting" (DD, IV, i).

It bears repeating that the marriages of Cynthia and Mellefont or Millamant and Mirabell do not imply a resolution to their argument. But neither do they involve a resignation which puts their desire behind them. Instead, these marriages can be seen as marking a certain rearrangement in their relationship to this desire. Congreve understands that it is not convention which represses desire by interposing artificial distances and differences between it and its object. It is desire which mystifies convention by making these differences the symbols of an impossible fulfillment. In this way lovers bind themselves to a sterile and reactive war against the inevitability of limitation.

It is this bondage, not the machinations of the Fainalls of the world, which is the real threat to Congreve's couples. The figures of the pleading lover and the reluctant woman are static, frozen in their respective gestures, lost in the contemplation of their own image. In their willingness to press their suits even after they have become aware of the inevitability of difference, in their willingness, in Mirabell's words, "to be made wise by the dictates of reason, and yet persevere to play the fool by the force of instinct" (WW, II, ii), these couples find a way to escape this kind of stasis.

This freedom means that they can now experience their desire productively. If the figures of the lovers are initially static, time is not. This is the danger which Mellefont sees in Cynthia's future.

> Prithee, Cynthia, look behind you,
> Age and wrinkles will o'ertake you;
> Then, too late, desire will find you,
> When the power must forsake you:
> Think, O think, 'o th' sad condition,
> To be past, yet wish fruition!
>
> (DD, II, i)

Finally, for Congreve beauty is not an image to be worshiped by the lover as a sign of his fulfillment or by the woman as a sign of her power. It is biological and therefore part of the material processes of life. It generates a desire which is not meant to be satisfied but to be used. When these couples accept the frustrations of their argument, it is not a sign of resignation. Instead, it allows them, for the first time, to express desire free of the imaginary goal of satisfaction. They can, in other words, desire the other and enter that play of differences which is the variety, if not the plenitude, of life.

# Notes

INTRODUCTION

1. Nancy K. Miller, *The Heroine's Text: Readings in the French and English Novel, 1722–1782* (New York: Columbia University Press, 1980). See particularly her epilogue, pp. 149–54.

2. Ibid., p. 3. Both Terry Eagleton's *The Rape of Clarissa: Writing, Sexuality and Class Struggle in Samuel Richardson* (Minneapolis: University of Minnesota Press, 1983) and Terry Castle's *Clarissa's Ciphers: Meaning and Disruption in Richardson's Clarissa* (Ithaca, N.Y.: Cornell University Press, 1983) take a similar approach. For an interesting analysis of this shift from theory to history, see William Warner's "Reading Rape: Marxist-Feminist Figurations of the Literal," *Diacritics* (forthcoming).

CHAPTER I

1. All quotations from the *Songs and Sonnets* are from the edition by Theodore Redpath, *The Songs and Sonets of John Donne* (London: Methuen, 1956). Where necessary, I have included the title along with the line number.

2. The place of married love in a tradition which has its origins in the celebration of extramarital love affairs, or their transformation into religious allegory, has always been an issue in discussions of English lyric poetry in the Renaissance. C. S. Lewis remarks that "the great central movement of love poetry, and of fiction about love, in Donne's time is that represented by Shakespeare and Spenser. This movement consisted in the final transmutation of the medieval courtly love or romance of adultery into a love that looked to marriage as its natural conclusion." ("Donne and Love Poetry in the Seventeenth Century," *Seventeenth-Century Studies Presented to Sir Herbert Grierson*, ed. J. Dover Wilson [Oxford: The Clarendon Press, 1938], p. 71.) Obviously, from this point of view couples such as Tom Jones and Sophia or B and Pamela represent the final step in this domestication of romantic love.

3. See Grierson's comments in his introductory essay entitled "The Poetry of John Donne," *The Poems of John Donne*, ed. Herbert

Grierson (Oxford: The Clarendon Press, 1912), vol. 2, pp. xxxiv–xlix.

4. See, for example, Helen Gardner's comments in the general introduction to her edition of the *Songs and Sonnets*. Speaking of this group of poems, she remarks that it is in these poems of mutual love that "Donne has no model and no rival, is at his most original and his greatest." General Introduction, *The Elegies and the Songs and Sonets* (Oxford: The Clarendon Press, 1965), p. xxviii. This connection between maturity and poetic achievement is a commonplace in traditional Donne criticism.

5. Grierson, in his commentary, warns against viewing the *Songs and Sonnets* as a development from cynical wit to maturity: "Moreover it is to conceive somewhat inadequately of Donne's complex nature to make too sharp a temporal division between his gayer, more cynical effusions and his graver, even religious, pieces. The truth of Donne is well stated by Professor Norton: 'Donne's "better angel" and his "worse spirit" seem to have kept up a continual contest, now the one, now the other, gaining the mastery in his "Poor soul, the center of his sinful earth." ' " *The Poems of John Donne*, vol. 2, pp. 8–9.

6. Lewis, "Donne and Love Poetry in the Seventeenth Century," *Seventeenth Century Studies*, pp. 64–84; and J. E. V. Crofts's "John Donne, *Essays and Studies by Members of the English Association*, vol. 22 (Oxford: The Clarendon Press, 1937), reprinted in *John Donne: A Collection of Critical Essays*, ed. Helen Gardner (Englewood Cliffs, N.J.: Prentice-Hall, 1962), pp. 77–90.

7. John Donne, "A Defence of Woman's Inconstancy," *Paradoxes and Problems*, in *Complete Poetry and Selected Prose*, ed. John Hayward (London: The Nonesuch Press, 1929), p. 103.

8. Lawrence Stone, *The Family, Sex and Marriage in England, 1500–1800* (New York: Harper & Row, 1979), p. 304.

9. Gardner, p. 174.

10. *Complete Poetry*, p. 89.

11. Ibid., p. 68

12. Ibid., p. 100. Gardner does not include this among Donne's poetry, but Grierson accepts it.

13. Ibid., p. 100.

14. For my present purposes, the two most useful essays by Julia Kristeva were "Le Geste: Pratique ou communication?" *Langages*, 10 (June 1968), 48–64, and "Le Sujet en procès," in *Polylogue* (Paris: Editions du Seuil, 1977), pp. 55–106.

15. Gardner, p. xxxv.

16. Stein, *John Donne's Lyrics* (Minneapolis, Minn: University of Minnesota Press, 1962), p. 72.

17. Stein, p. 73.

18. Farwell, "Virginia Woolf and Androgyny," *Contemporary Literature*, 16 (1975), 434. A number of other female critics view this image in the same way. See, for example, the issue of *Women's Studies* devoted to androgny (*Women's Studies*, 2, no. 2 [1974]).

19. Farwell, p. 435.

20. Farwell, pp. 436–37.

21. Stein, p. 76.

22. Sanders, *John Donne's Poetry* (London: Cambridge University Press, 1971), pp. 67–68.

23. Stein, p. 75.

## CHAPTER II

1. Kronhausen, *Pornography and the Law* (New York: Ballantine Books, 1964), p. 114.

2. Malcolm Bradbury, "*Fanny Hill* and the Comic Novel," *Critical Quarterly*, XIII (1971) 265–275.

3. Geoffrey Gorer, *Does Pornography Matter?* ed. Cecil R. Hewitt (London: Routledge & Kegan Paul, 1961), p. 98.

4. This issue has two aspects. One is historical and involves the appearance in the eighteenth century not only of commercial pornography, such as *Fanny Hill*, but of a whole literature of fantasy designed to appeal to the tastes of a readership which was increasingly literate but decreasingly learned. The standard work on the origin of pornography in eighteenth-century England is David Foxton's *Libertine Literature in England, 1660–1745* (New York: University Books, 1965). Donald Thomas, in *A Long Time Burning: A History of Literary Censorship in England* (London: Praeger, 1969), provides interesting background material on the prosecution of *Fanny Hill*. John Atkins's *Sex in Literature* (New York: Grove Press, 1972) provides a valuable survey of erotic literature and allows the reader to develop some sense of the differences among the erotic, the pornographic, and the bawdy.

On the relationship between *Fanny Hill* and the popular literature of fantasy, see John J. Richetti's *Popular Fiction before Richardson* (Oxford: The Clarendon Press, 1969). Richetti's discussions of whore and rogue biographies and, particularly, of the erotic appeal of the works of Mrs. Manley and Mrs. Heywood, allow us to see how much *Fanny Hill* is a part of the literature of its time.

The second aspect is, loosely speaking, theoretical and has to do with the significance of the reader's experience of pornography. Two articles which address this issue in ways particularly relevant to my discussion are Taylor Stoehr's "Pornography, Masturbation and the Novel," *Salmagundi*, 2 (1967–68) 28–56, and Susan Sontag's "The Pornographic Imagination," *Partisan Review*, 2 (1967), 35–73. Stoehr's essay is a review of Steven Marcus's *The Other Victorians* but develops another, larger thesis concerning the relation of pornography and the Gothic novel. At the very least, Stoehr's argument makes clear, on the one hand, that it is artificial and silly to talk about pornography without discussing the experience of masturbation, and, on the other, that this experience is not unrelated to the appeal of more respectable themes such as the Gothic and the sublime. Sontag's essay deals with the seriousness of pornography, which she finds in the way it criticizes and undermines conservative literary structures and the idea of the coherent, historical, unified subject implied by them. Her discussion is an attempt to invoke a French tradition of intellectual pornography represented by Sade, Bataille, and Artaud. My own discussion, obviously, owes a great deal to this approach.

5. B. Slepian and L. J. Morrissey, "What is *Fanny Hill*?" *Essays in Criticism*, 14 (1964), 65–75.

6. See John Hollander, "The Old Last Act," *Encounter*, 22 (1963), 69–77, and Bradbury, "*Fanny Hill* and the Comic Novel."

7. See Nancy K. Miller's " 'I's' in Drag: The Sex of Recollection," *The Eighteenth Century*, 20 (1981), 45–57. Miller's article is an interesting critique of any simple acceptance of the apparent "femocentricism" of the eighteenth-century novel. She argues that the masculine assumption of the feminine voice in novels such as *Fanny Hill* and *Manon Lescaut* is always accomplished in such a way that reaffirms phallic structures of domination and authority. My own argument, of course, tries to locate an experience of the work which escapes this kind of recuperation.

8. Gloria Steinem's comment that "it's violence and domination that are pornographic . . . Pornography is the instruction; rape is the practice" (quoted in Leslie Bennett's article "Conference Examines Pornography as a Feminist Issue," New York *Times*, September 17, 1979, p. B10) is as good a summary of this position as any. Steinem argues elsewhere for a clear distinction between the pornographic, which always involves violence, and the erotic, which never does. For an equivalent argument directed specifically at those male French thinkers—Barthes and Sollers among them—who assert the radical and liberating effect of pornography in the tradition of Bataille and Sade, see Benoîte Groult's "Les Portiers du nuit" in *Ainsi soit-elle* (Paris: Grasset, 1975) a portion of which is included in Elaine Marks and

Isabelle de Courtivron, eds., *New French Feminisms* (New York: Schocken Books, 1981), pp. 68–75. For Groult pornography always invokes a desire for "that which is dirty, degrading, and destructive, which is to say for death." For this reason it is "an extension of the bourgeois . . . [which speaks] to a nostalgia for violence and domination felt by more men than one would think" (pp. 69 and 72–73, respectively). My own position is closer to that of Diana George (see note 10 below). To anticipate my argument, I suggest that *Fanny Hill* attempts to undercut the fixed difference between male and female by playing on the ambivalence of both sexes—the capacity which both men and women possess for adopting both masculine and feminine attitudes to their experience. The reciprocity which results does not escape difference but rather attenuates it, destroys, in Steinem's terms, the barriers to empathy which exist between the sexes. This relativization of the opposition masculine/feminine, an opposition which can now be experienced fully by both men and women, leads, in turn, to an idea of mutual understanding which characterizes the relation of Fanny and Charles at the end of the novel. Since this is a sensitive area, I would like to emphasize, first, that I am making this argument in the context of a reading of *Fanny Hill* and not in relation to pornography in general, and, second, that it is not a position which I agree with in the terms Cleland presents it. I am simply formulating this possibility as it exists in the novel—a formulation which, it seems to me, not only characterizes a certain plateau in the relationship of many couples but also has some theoretical currency now. See, for example, June Singer, *Androgyny: Toward a New Theory of Sexuality* (Garden City, N.Y.: Doubleday/Anchor Press, 1976).

9. *Les Liaisons dangereuses* provides one of the clearest examples of the way an apparently "liberated" attitude toward sexuality does not imply a liberated attitude toward women. It is a world in which men are ennobled by affairs and women are ruined by them. Consequently the libertine world simply reproduces the same domination of women by men that characterizes the bourgeois world. For this reason it is perfectly possible for Valmont to adopt a relaxed attitude toward pleasure, to surrender to its effects, because this surrender can always be recuperated as power at any time. Mme. de Merteuil, on the other hand, can never relax.

10. Diana Hume George, "The Myth of Mythlessness and the New Mythology of Love: Feminist Theory on Rape and Pornography," *Enclitic*, 4, no. 2 (1983), 35.

11. George, p. 41.

12. All quotations are from the Dell/Putnam edition of *Fanny Hill*,

edited by Peter Quennell (New York, 1963), since this is the most widely circulated edition. I have indicated page numbers in parentheses after the quotation.

13. The relation between the pornographic and the visual has been the subject of much critical attention lately. Perhaps the central essay on this issue is Laura Mulvey's "Visual Pleasure and Narrative Cinema," *Screen*, 16 (1975), 6–18. Mulvey's article attempts to chart the spectator's position in relation to two pairs of oppositions: first, the difference between a dominating scopophilia which enjoys the power of looking and a narcissistic scopophilia which identifies with the subject of the gaze; and, second, the difference between voyeurism and fetishism as it defines the spectator's fascination with the image of the woman in film. Mulvey's analysis of the spectator's position is complex but for her the structures of viewing in cinema—structures which are essentially similar to the narrative point of view in *Fanny Hill*—ultimately always support masculine fantasies of voyeuristic omnipotence and fetishistic presence. Although, in the case of fetishistic viewing, she allows a certain identification between the viewer and the object, it is an identification which implies the suppression of the feminine, of castration.

Mulvey, of course, is writing about films which are, for the most part, viewed in a public context. While her argument does bear on literary pornography, it is understandable that she does not concern herself with film's private use.

14. See also pp. 89–90, where Will demonstrates an equivalent male fascination with the vagina. For an interesting analysis of pornography's obsession with women's genitals, see John Ellis's "Photography/Pornography/Art/Pornography," *Screen*, 21 (1980), 81–109.

15. Leo Bersani includes an enlightening discussion of this issue in *Freud and Baudelaire* (Berkeley: Quantum, 1977), pp. 38ff.

16. The appropriate context for this inversion of the voyeuristic is Freud's discussion of scopophilia in connection with the genesis of sadism and masochism in "Instincts and their Vicissitudes" and his later development of an idea of primary masochism in "The Economic Problem of Masochism" and "Beyond the Pleasure Principle." Bersani presents an interesting discussion of these issues in *Freud and Baudelaire*, pp. 75–85, which focuses specifically on moments in which voyeurism is eroticized in a way destructive to the structured subject. Bersani here is reading Freud by way of Jean Laplanche's *Life and Death in Psychoanalysis*, trans. Jeffrey Mehlman (Baltimore, Md.: The Johns Hopkins University Press, 1976).

17. This formulation of the opposition between the thematic and

the erotic draws heavily on Kristeva's analysis of Bataille in her essay "L'Expérience et la pratique," *Polylogue* (Paris: Editions du Seuil, 1977), pp. 107–36.

18. One of the most interesting discussions of the difference between the idea of sexual experience as a kind of absolute violence, on the one hand, and as specific and various pleasures, on the other, is found in Jane Gallop's discussion of Bataille's reading of Sade in her *Intersections* (Lincoln, Nebr.: University of Nebraska Press, 1981), pp. 29–33. She locates this distinction in the difference between *volupté* and *agrément*. "*Volupté*, with its emphasis on intensity, maintains the unity and selfsameness of 'sexual pleasure,' which unlike other pleasures needs no qualifications, is always identical in its pure intensity" (pp. 31–32). It is a kind of negative ideal of masculine visions of coherence and unity which can be experienced only as pure destruction. The woman, then, becomes the mark of this destruction and must be mastered. The man must distance himself from pleasure and reduce the woman to the object of a voyeuristic gaze. So the loss of sexual experience is recuperated as the proof of mastery and authority. In contrast, *agrément* designates a relationship to experience which escapes conventional economics by pluralizing pleasure and making its relation to the subject immediate. "The definition of *agrément* slides from a proper subservience to authority into a general insubordination to any rule, even that of one's own interests. The central definition (agreeableness that is inherent in an object), which appears to have no relation to permission or approval, is actually a turning point in the relation to some transcendent hierarchic principle which would subordinate to its own ends any charm that is merely imminent in the thing. The moment of innocent pleasantness marks the start of a perverse insubordination to any external authority or approval. The possibility for simple, self-contained pleasure which makes no reference to permission or morality is the germ of explicit opposition to utility . . ." (p. 31). In my reading, it is this second, agreeable, pleasure which characterizes Fanny's life at Mrs. Cole's.

Bearing this distinction in mind, the difference between masculine and feminine shifts from a conventional relationship to anatomical difference and depends instead on the subject's experience of the body in pleasure. See, for example, Hélène Cixous's comments in her essay "Sorties" in *La Jeune née* (Paris: Union Générale d'Editions, 1975), excerpted in *New French Feminisms*, pp. 90–98. Sexual difference, she writes, "is not determined merely by the fantasized relationship to anatomy, which is based, to a great extent, upon the point of *view*, therefore upon a strange importance accorded (by Freud and Lacan) to exteriority and to the specular elaboration of sexuality. A voyeur's theory, of course. No, it is at the level of sexual pleasure [*jouissance*] in my opinion, that the difference makes itself most clearly apparent . . ." (p. 95).

At this level it is at least theoretically possible for a male subject to move from a masculine to a feminine relationship to pleasure just as *Fanny Hill* seems to lead the reader from a masculine position of voyeurism to a feminine experience of a blind and immediate rapture. Again, I want to emphasize that this kind of male identification with a feminine self does not necessarily escape the difference between the sexes. On the other hand, it seems to me that Cleland believed that it did, and that for him masculine and feminine designated two poles of a continuous range of attitudes toward experience which were, potentially at least, open to both sexes.

19. The argument, at this level, might seem either too theoretical or too individual. But in Barbara Ehrenreich's recent book *The Hearts of Men* (Garden City, N.Y.: Doubleday/Anchor Books, 1983), a history of male consciousness from the 1950s through the present, this distinction between masculine and feminine relations to pleasure appears a larger context. Discussing the movement away from traditional masculine ideals toward a more androgynous sensibility in the post-Vietnam era, she quotes from the autobiography of Charles Reich, whose *The Greening of America* was at that time read as a prophetic text. In this passage Reich describes his experience of lunch in the world of macho lawyers.

> The dishes were excellent: soft-shelled crabs, imported English sole, crab-meat au gratin . . . I would have liked to add an extra vegetable . . . but I held back . . . I quailed at drawing attention to the fact that I was specifically interested in the food itself . . . What I really wanted, at this particular moment, was to savor the lobster bisque . . . But once the food arrived, everyone showed a total unconcern about it. They sawed away at their filet of sole or other dishes as if they were meat and potatoes at a highway roadhouse. (Ehrenreich, p. 110)

In this world even the minor disturbance created by the pleasure of good food must be rigidly suppressed. The dishes become simply the sign of masculine values of affluence and power. Later, however, Reich moves to college teaching, where he becomes the student of his students. "They did not find it unmanly," Ehrenreich comments, "to revel in the sensual immediacy of things" (p. 111).

In this way Reich is freed from the prison of traditional masculine roles to deliver himself to the bisque. Ehrenreich's analysis reveals how much this new male openness to pleasure lies not only behind alternative lifestyles but also behind the emergence of the *Playboy* ideal of the man who enjoys and, more generally, the explosion of pornography in the 1970s. "Outside of professional literature," Ehrenreich notes, "the critique of the male sex role can be found in a surprising variety of 'low-brow' publications—for example, pornographic magazines. Contrary to the conviction held by some feminists that pornography is an unrelieved incitement to male sexual aggression, porn magazines do not hesitate to attack the male 'role' when it threatens to inhibit male sexual inclinations, no matter how peculiar" (pp. 125-26). As an example, she cites the letter to *Response* from a young woman who writes to complain that her boyfriend, Dwight, likes to be dressed as a woman and called Diane. In her letter the girl complains that she isn't offended by this but that sometimes she would like someone to take care of her. The magazine replies, "Psychologists and psychiatrists agree that men sometimes get tired of role-playing . . . This is obviously what you've run into in Dwight/Diane— a guy who . . . isn't interested in 'proving' what the rest of the world thinks of as 'his' masculinity all the time" (p. 126).

From this point of view, *Fanny Hill*'s emphasis on seducing readers into a feminine surrender to pleasure which takes them outside traditional masculine attitudes would seem to locate one important element—not *the* most important element—in men's relation to pornography itself, which provides a secret access to this kind of experience. On the other hand, the relationship between this experience and the nature of even the most liberated pornography does show how a man's acceptance of "feminine" pleasure does not imply that he will adopt feminist attitudes.

CHAPTER III

1. Leo Braudy, "The Form of the Sentimental Novel," *Novel*, 6 (Fall 1973), 6.

2. Malcolm Bradbury, "*Fanny Hill* and the Comic Novel," *Critical Quarterly*, 13 (1971), 265.

3. Richard Kuhns, "The Beautiful and the Sublime," *New Literary History*, 13 (1982), 293.

4. Kuhns, pp. 288-307.

5. *The Correspondence of Samuel Richardson*, ed. A. L. Barbauld (New York: AMS Press, 1966), vol. 3, pp. 244-46. All references to Richardson's letters (abbreviated in text as C) are to this edition. For a study of the role of Richardson's correspondence in his life, see

Marvin R. Zirker, Jr., "Richardson's Correspondence: The Personal Letter as Private Experience" in *The Familiar Letter in the 18th Century*, ed. Howard Anderson, Philip Daghlian, and Irving Ehrenpreis (Lawrence, Kan.: University of Kansas Press, 1966), pp. 71–91.

6. Samuel Richardson, *Pamela* (New York: Norton, 1958), p. 272. All references to *Pamela* are to this edition.

7. Samuel Richardson, *Clarissa* (New York: Dutton, 1948), vol. 2, p. 375. All references to *Clarissa* are to this edition.

8. For a recent reading from an alternative perspective, see Terry J. Castle's "P/B: *Pamela* as Sexual Fiction," *Studies in English Literature*, 22 (1982), pp. 469–89. Castle reads *Pamela* as the story of a young girl's passage through the Oedipal. This is a perfectly reasonable approach. But any interpretation of the novel which makes B the simple sign of the masculine is being a little naive about his position. For an article which puts B's discomfort in historical perspective, see Patricia Spack's "Early Fiction and the Frightened Male," *Novel*, 7 (Fall 1974), 8–17. John Dussinger's "What Pamela Knew: An Interpretation," *Journal of English and Germanic Philology*, 69 (1970), 377–93, gives B's side of the Oedipal drama.

9. Lawrence Stone, *The Family, Sex and Marriage in England, 1500–1800* (New York: Harper & Row, 1977). See, particularly, Part IV, pp. 149–303.

10. Jean H. Hagstrum, *Sex and Sensibility: Ideal and Erotic Love from Milton to Mozart* (Chicago: University of Chicago Press, 1980).

11. Stone, pp. 218–19.

12. Hagstrum's interpretation restates and extends the point of view of much scholarly commentary on English love poetry of the Renaissance—and on Donne and Spenser particularly—commentary which emphasizes the adaptation of platonic and courtly motifs to a human and domestic situation. In his commitment to this ideal, Hagstrum is as uncomfortable as Richardson himself with a sexuality which violates limits, and his book is least satisfying when he is dealing with, for example, the relation of love and death. On the other hand, he is particularly eloquent when he discusses Pamela's physicality and its effect on B (pp. 195–97), a discussion which makes it clear that while she may be silent, she cannot be described as passive.

13. For an interesting treatment of this issue, see Jane Gallop's analysis of the "ladies' man" in *The Daughter's Seduction: Feminism and Psychoanalysis* (Ithaca, N.Y.: Cornell University Press, 1982), pp. 33–42.

CHAPTER IV

1. Choderlos de Laclos, *Les Liaisons dangereuses*, trans. P. W. K. Stone (Harmondsworth, England: Penguin, 1961). All quotations are from this translation, which is the most widely available. To make it easier to refer to the original, or to other translations, I have given the number of the letter in parentheses after each quotation.

2. Said's discussion of irony and its relation to the principles of authority and molestation occurs in the third chapter of *Beginnings: Intention and Method* (Baltimore, Md.: The Johns Hopkins University Press, 1975). My discussion here places Merteuil and the question of irony in the context of a certain approach to the theme of the novel as a genre. An equally valuable approach is suggested by Thomas Fries's analysis of the relation between irony and the feminine in "The Impossible Object: The Feminine, The Narrative (Laclos' *Liaisons Dangereuses* and Kleist's Marquise von O . . .)," *Modern Language Notes*, 91 (1976), 1296–1326. Fries is interested particularly in the relation between *Les Liaison dangereuses* and Laclos's essays on the education of women.

3. Ibid. p. 82.

4. Ibid. p. 87.

5. For a more extended—and more sophisticated—discussion of these issues, see Ramon Saldivar's essay "Don Quijote's Metaphors and the Grammar of Proper Language," *Modern Language Notes*, 95 (1980), 252–78.

6. Any study of the complicated relation between Laclos's novel and the particular conventions of eighteenth-century life should begin with Laurent Versani's *Laclos et la tradition* (Paris: Klincksieck, 1968); it should also include Peter Brooks's *The Novel of Worldliness* (Princeton: Princeton University Press, 1969) and a study I found particularly helpful, Philip Stewart's *Le Masque et la parole* (Paris: Corti, 1973). Any interpretation of *Les Liaisons dangereuses* should acknowledge Tsvetan Todorov's important reading of the novel in *Littérature et signification* (Paris: Larousse, 1967), as well as Jean-Luc Seylaz's *Les Liaisons dangereuses et la création romanesque chez Laclos* (Geneva: Gallimard, 1958).

7. Nancy K. Miller, in *The Heroine's Text: Readings in the French and English Novel, 1722–1782* (New York: Columbia University Press, 1980), is particularly eloquent on Merteuil's position. See also her review article of Pierre Fauchery's *La Destinée féminine dans le roman Européen du dix-huitième siècle 1713–1807: Essai de gynecomythe romanesque* (Paris: Armand Colin, 1972). In the latter she is par-

ticularly perceptive about the way Fauchery's ambivalent celebration of Merteuil's fate disguises his complicity in the novel's reaffirmation of masculine power.

8. My comments here are directed not so much at any specific critic but at the tendency of any interpretation—my own included—to become a metalanguage which seduces by its apparent ability to allow the critic to transcend the conditions of the text. Irving Wohlfarth's essay (see n. 10), a reading of the major critics of Laclos, addresses this issue directly.

9. Foucault, in the first volume of his *Histoire de la sexualité* (Paris: Gallimard, 1976), insists that power is strictly relational in nature. Power, in other words, is not an entity which can be owned but a force exerted against something which, in turn, resists. Gossip can be seen, in Foucault's terms, as a discourse which manifests the power of convention to control sexuality. But gossip also titillates, creates areas of intense sexuality, and becomes, in the hands of Merteuil and Valmont, an eroticized power.

10. Irving Wohlfarth offers an interesting reading of the position of the editor in his article "The Irony of Criticism of Irony: A Study of Laclos Criticism," *Studies on Voltaire and the Eighteenth Century*, 120 (1974), 269–317. Wohlfarth argues against the idea that the editor is, in fact, a disguised author whose controlling position makes him a "Valmont of composition" and validates the ironic mastery of the *libertin*. His study is particularly interesting in the way it shows how most major critics of the novel have been led to repeat this mystification, to identify with this Valmont-like author, by their own desire for mastery and control of the text. This is an identification which, from the point of view of my reading, the editor explicitly warns against. See also Ronald C. Rosbottom's comments on the problematic of reading the novel in his *Choderlos de Laclos* (Boston: Twayne, 1978), pp. 94–113.

CHAPTER V

1. For the former see Aubrey L. Williams's *An Approach to Congreve* (New Haven, Conn.: Yale University Press, 1979). Williams is committed to reading Congreve within the context of traditional Renaissance and eighteenth-century patterns of Christian allegory. His comments at the beginning of his chapter on *The Way of the World* (pp. 192–93) defend Mirabell against the interpretations of recent critics who read him as an amoral manipulator. See, for example, W. H. Van Voris, *The Cultivated Stance* (Chester Springs, Pa.: Dufor Editions, 1965); Ian Donaldson, *The World Upside-Down*,

(Oxford: The Clarendon Press, 1970); Harold Love, *Congreve* (Oxford: Blackwell, 1974). These readers emphasize Mirabell's practical ability to reconcile "the contradictory pressures of affection, kinship and law" (Love, p. 106). This opposition defines the range of contemporary readings of Congreve.

My own approach is dictated by the nature of my argument throughout this book and consequently focuses somewhat narrowly on the relation of lovers as a function of their imaginary relation to one another. In this context the questions of the lover's sincerity and the reconciliation of the individual and society take on their own resonances. Because my own is such a specialized—even idiosyncratic—approach, I have allowed it to play itself out without attempting to relate it specifically to the more comprehensive views of other critics.

2. All quotations are from *William Congreve: Complete Plays*, ed. A. C. Ewald (New York: Hill & Wang, 1956). I have given the play, act, and scene following each excerpt. For the sake of simplicity, I have abbreviated the titles as follows:

TOB    *The Old Bachelor*
DD     *The Double-Dealer*
LL     *Love for Love*
WW     *The Way of the World*

3. On this motif in Ariosto's work, see Eugenio Donato's " 'Per Selve e Boscherecci Labirinti': Desire and Narrative Structure in Ariosto's *Orlando Furioso*," *Barroco*, 4 (1973), 17–34. On the analogy between the image of the woman in lyric poetry and the circulation of money in a modern economy, I found Eugene Vance's "Love's Concordance: The Poetics of Desire and the Joy of the Text," *Diacritics*, 5 (1975), 40–52, particularly helpful.

# Index